THE BOOK OF SNUBS

By the same editor

The Politician's Quotation Book

The Book of Snubs

Edited by

GYLES BRANDRETH

St. Martin's Press ❧ New York

THE BOOK OF SNUBS. Copyright © 1994 by Gyles Brandreth.
All rights reserved. Printed in the United States of
America. No part of this book may be used or reproduced
in any manner whatsoever without written permission
except in the case of brief quotations embodied in critical
articles or reviews. For information, address St. Martin's Press,
175 Fifth Avenue, New York, N.Y. 10010.

Library of Congress Cataloging-in-Publication Data
The Book of snubs / Gyles Brandreth, editor.
p.   cm.
"A Thomas Dunne book."
ISBN 0-312-13442-8
1. Celebrities—Quotations, maxims, etc.   I. Brandreth, Gyles
Daubeney, 1948-   .
PN6084.C44B66   1995
082—dc20   95-32885   CIP

First published in Great Britain by Robert Hale

First U.S. Edition: October 1995
10 9 8 7 6 5 4 3 2 1

Preface

Only twice in my life have I bought books by the yard. In Edinburgh about twenty years ago I acquired the *Complete Works of William Makepeace Thackeray* in twenty-two volumes (Smith, Elder edition, 1867–69, 3 ft 6 ins), and, later the same year, I splashed out on the seventeen volumes of the *Oxford English Dictionary* (3 ft 8 ins including Supplements). Of course, I have not read all of Thackeray, let alone more than half an inch of the OED, but I have dipped extensively into both, and the former's *Book of Snobs* helped me towards a title for this little collection while the latter's Volume IX has provided me with the authoritative definition of what it is intended to contain.

Snub (*noun*): a remark or action intended to repress or rebuke a person.

Snub (*verb*): to check, reprove or rebuke in a sharp or cutting manner, to treat or receive (a person or suggestion, etc.) in a way calculated to repress or mortify.

Given that Henry VIII was a monarch notorious for his rebukes in the 'cutting manner' it is appropriate that the first written use of the word 'snub' comes from Archbishop Cranmer in the State Papers of King Henry in 1537. The OED also cites Bunyan (1688), Congreve (1694), Richardson (1748), and the *Saturday Review* of 14 September 1861: 'When we endeavour to analyse it, the immediate effect of a snub is to induce a feeling of deprivation and exposure.'

Thackeray, of course, was concerned with snobs rather than snubs, but he was keenly aware that the former frequently deployed the latter. Ivor Brown, in one of his delightful excursions into the byways of the English language (*Just Another Word*, 1943), pointed out that words beginning with 'sn' frequently betray contempt:

> When the snob is spurning or rebuking his supposed inferiors, he conforms to the habit of his first letters. Here is a catalogue of proud, contemptuous 'sn's' – sneer, snib, snicker, sniff, sneap, snotty or snooty, snub, snuffy. Sneap is the most dignified of these, a word of pedigree as well as of pride. Falstaff used sneap for rebuke: 'I will not undergo this sneap without reply.'

For a snob of the first order who could deliver a sneap of the first degree, you would be hard put to better George Nathaniel Curzon, Viceroy of India, Foreign Secretary and, in 1921, Chancellor of Oxford University, when Queen Mary was to be entertained at his old college, Balliol. Curzon was invited to approve the proposed menu in advance of the royal visit. He returned it to the hapless College Bursar with the single comment: 'Gentlemen do not take soup at luncheon.'

Whether delivered face to face, or scrawled on the foot of a menu card, a snub is only a true snub when there is a vulnerable victim as well as a polished perpetrator. James McNeill Whistler, the celebrated American painter, is one of those seasoned exponents of the snub-direct who features frequently in the pages that follow, although not on account of the line he delivered at the expense of Sir Redvers Buller at the time of the Boer War. The story goes that at a dinner party fellow guests were lauding the action of Buller who, as British commander, had retreated across the Modder River 'without losing a man, a flag or a gun.' 'Or a minute,' added Whistler.

Had Buller been at the dinner, Whistler's put-down could have been classified as a snub. As the gallant officer was not present to receive the rebuke personally, it must count as a sneer rather than a snub.

Whistler's most celebrated remark was addressed to Oscar Wilde. When the painter had said something particularly witty, Wilde sighed, 'Oh, I wish I'd said that.' Whistler retorted, 'You will, Oscar, you will.' And he probably did. Apart from constantly wrestling with the issue of when is a snub truly a snub, the other challenge facing the compiler of a collection like this is: who said it? And who said it first? Some of the best lines attributed to Whistler have also been attributed to Oscar Wilde or Bernard Shaw or Mark Twain.

Several of the snubs that I have attributed to the great F.E. Smith I have seen attributed to other eminent lawyers, including Edward Carson and Norman Birkett. Certainly Smith had few equals, and no betters, as a master of the courtroom put-down. He could be charming:

Mr Justice Darling: And who is George Robey?
F.E: Mr George Robey is the Darling of the music-halls, m'lud.

More often, he would be caustic:

Judge: I have read your case, Mr Smith, and I am no wiser now than I was when I started.

F.E: Possibly not, my lord, but far better informed.

The most celebrated of his courtroom rallies took place with the well-intentioned but long-winded Judge Willis in Southwark County Court. A boy had been run over by a tram and was suing the tramway company for damages on the grounds that the accident had led to his blindness. The judge was affected by the lad's plight: 'Poor, poor boy! Blind! Put him on a chair so the jury can see him.'

F.E. was appearing for the tramway company and protested: 'Perhaps your honour would like to have the boy passed round the jury box?'

'That is a most improper remark,' reproved the judge.

'It was provoked by a most improper suggestion,' retorted F.E.

Judge Willis paused and then offered the outspoken counsel a lofty rebuke: 'Mr Smith, have you ever heard of a saying by Bacon – the great Bacon – that youth and discretion are ill-wedded companions?'

'Indeed I have, your honour,' came the instant reply. 'And has your honour ever heard of a saying by Bacon – the great Bacon – that a much-talking judge is like an ill-tuned cymbal?'

'You are extremely offensive,' spluttered the hapless Willis.

'As a matter of fact,' demurred F.E., 'we both are; the difference between us is that I'm trying to be and you can't help it.'

On another occasion the same unfortunate judge turned testily to F.E. and remarked, 'What do you suppose I am on the bench for, Mr Smith?' F.E.'s rejoinder was immediate and devastating: 'It is not for me, your honour, to attempt to fathom the inscrutable workings of Providence.'

I hope my readers will forgive the occasional incorrect attribution and will understand that in certain instances attribution of any kind has proved impossible. Here is a story for which I would be grateful for verification. At a formal embassy dinner a few years ago all the guests had been seated and grace had been said when one of the ladies complained that, according to the correct order of precedence, she should have been seated next to the ambassador. There were some discreet whispered consultations and it was acknowledged that a mistake had indeed been made. One whole side of the table had to rise and move along in order that the lady should take her rightful place at the ambassador's side. When the room had returned to order she turned to her host and apologized: 'I expect you and your wife find these questions of protocol quite troublesome?' 'Not really,' replied his excellency. 'You see we have found from experience that those people who matter don't mind, and those people that mind don't matter.'

The snub is so telling, and the victim so deserving, that it would be good to be able to name names and give credit where it is due.

'Going so soon,' trilled the anonymous hostess as the unhappy guest attempted to make a discreet escape. 'Do you really have to leave?'

'I don't have to,' came the curt response. 'It is merely a matter of choice.'

The collection that follows is also merely a matter of choice. I have made a personal selection of snubs of every variety, some real, some imagined, some from life, some from literature; most, I hope, legitimate snubs, what one might term ur-snubs, according strictly with the OED definition; a few, more marginal, um-er-snubs, here simply because I couldn't resist them. I hope my choice meets with your approval. If it doesn't, perhaps you will let me know. Or perhaps you won't. Who said, 'Silence is the unbearable repartee'?

Richard Porson, a contemporary of Dr Johnson, was a noted scholar of Trinity College, Cambridge, and Regius professor of Greek. His scholarship on the plays of Euripides was second to none. A young Fellow at Trinity had the temerity to suggest that he and Porson might write a book together on the Greek tragedies, provoking the response:

'Put in all I know and all you don't know and it will be a great work.'

Porson and John Gillies, who had written a *History of Ancient Greece*, were discussing Greek poetry. Gillies was forthright in his opinion:

'We know nothing of the Greek metres.'

Porson was equally forthright in his response:

'If, Doctor, you will put your observation in the singular number, I believe it will be very accurate.'

Edward Thurlow rose to be Lord Chancellor at the end of the eighteenth century but at Cambridge he had been considered feckless and unpromising. His tutor rebuked him saying:

'Sir, I never come to the window but I see you idling in the court.'

Which prompted Thurlow's reply:

'Sir, I never come into the court but I see you idling at the window.'

Like many very brilliant men the nineteenth-century classical scholar W.H. Thompson did not suffer fools gladly. When fellow academic, Oscar Browning, complained to Thompson that he had so many books he did not know what to do with them, Thompson suggested:

'You might try reading them.'

The lawyer F.E. Smith long harboured a grudge against the professor who decided that Smith should not be awarded a first class degree after hearing his *viva voce* examination at Oxford. Many years later F.E., who was appointed Lord Chancellor at the extraordinarily early age of forty-seven, was asked to grant Silk to this same man who was applying to become a King's Counsel. It gave the Lord Chancellor great satisfaction to turn down this application with the words:

'Silk is only awarded to academic lawyers of distinction.

Early in this century the Master of Balliol would assemble the undergraduates at the end of term for what was called, and is still called, 'handshaking'. It was a ceremony at which he assessed the performance of each student in the presence of all the others. There was a young man who was universally disliked for his pomposity and conceit, and when the Master began:

'Mr Wilkins, I consider you the most brilliant man in college', there was a shudder throughout the hall, '... of your year', the Master continued (that was better), '... who is reading for Holy Orders', (there was only one other), the hall erupted in delight.

NIGEL NICOLSON
The Spectator, February 1994

On a visit to America Albert Einstein's wife was given a guided tour of the Mt. Wilson Observatory in California. Her guide showed her over the giant telescope and the leading astronomer took time to tell her how the complex machinery worked.

'One of the principal functions of all this sophisticated machinery,' he explained, 'is to find out the extent and shape of the universe.'

'Oh, my husband does that on the back of an old envelope,' was her ingenuous response.

I like pictures without knowing anything about them; but I hate coxcombry in the fine arts, as well as in everything else. I got into dreadful disgrace with Sir George Beaumont, who, standing before a picture at Bowood, exclaimed, turning to me:

'Immense breadth of light and shade!'

I innocently said:

'Yes; about an inch and a half.' He gave me a look that ought to have killed me.

SYDNEY SMITH
Memoirs and Letters of the Revd Sydney Smith,
1861

William Morris visited Paris shortly after the completion of the Eiffel Tower in 1889. During his stay he spent most of the hours of daylight at the tower. He ate all his meals there and occupied himself with painting and sketching. Gratified by this interest one of the staff approached him:

'You are certainly impressed with our tower, monsieur.'

'Impressed!' expostulated Morris. 'It's the only place in Paris where I can avoid seeing the damned thing.'

James Whistler, the noted nineteenth-century American artist, was driven by the desire to experiment, and had little time for the sentimental paintings so popular with his contemporaries. A wealthy art patron who wished to leave a bequest to a charitable foundation asked Whistler for his advice, expecting Whistler to draw up a list of paintings suitable for inclusion. Whistler's advice was more trenchant:

'I should leave them all to an asylum for the blind.'

Whistler was equally uncompromising with his paying customers, who might reasonably have expected a more accommodating approach. A man who had commissioned a portrait was deeply disappointed with the results.

Client: 'Do you call that a good piece of art?'

Whistler: 'Do you call yourself a good piece of nature?'

Mark Twain was invited by Whistler to visit his studio. Twain spent some time looking through the many canvases stacked along the walls and then turned his attention to the work in progress on the artist's easel. Reaching out he began to touch the surface of the paint, which was freshly applied.

'Stop!' cried Whistler. 'Can't you see the paint is still wet?'

'Oh don't worry,' said Twain, 'I have gloves on.'

The American art collector Louisine Havemeyer, much of whose collection was bequeathed to the Metropolitan Museum of Art in New York, was annoyed when quizzed by a wealthy matron as to why she spent her money on paint and canvas instead of the more reliable investment of good, expensive jewellery. Her inquisitor was naturally bedecked in prodigious quantities of jewels. Mrs Havemeyer looked the woman over, and having spent some time examining her much-prized strings of pearls declared:

'I find I prefer something made by man to something made by an oyster.'

Walter Sickert and Wyndham Lewis were at a dinner party. Over coffee Sickert offered Wyndham Lewis a cigar with the words:

'I offer you this cigar because I am a great admirer of your novels.' This cheered Wyndham Lewis, who had felt rather overshadowed during the meal. However the effect did not last long for Sickert continued:

'If I had liked your paintings I should have given you a bigger one.'

Dorothy Parker and Elsa Maxwell, American gossip columnist and hostess, were lunching with an art snob who was determined to make Elsa Maxwell feel self-conscious about her lack of culture. Having delivered a series of pompous put-downs, the man raised the topic of the work of Augustus John, making it clear that he and John were on intimate terms.

'Of course,' he said, turning to Maxwell, 'I don't suppose you know who I mean by Augustus John.'

'Oh yes she does,' piped up Dorothy Parker, 'only they're such great friends she knows him as Augustus Jack.'

Coming face to face with Beau Brummell in a busy street Sydney Smith stepped off the pavement to let him and his coterie sweep past. As an afterthought Beau Brummell called back:

'I never give way to fools.'

'I *always* do,' smiled Smith.

Lady Blessington was forced by debt and scandal to leave London and live in Paris. Having entertained the exiled Napoleon III many times in London she naturally expected recognition from the newly restored Emperor in Paris. However it became apparent that the Emperor wished to distance himself from Lady Blessington and her scandal-filled life. Eventually they met at a reception and Napoleon was obliged to speak to her.

'Lady Blessington,' he said formally, 'do you expect to stay long in Paris?'

Lady Blessington curtsied low and replied:

'Do you?'

The Ball at the Mansion House

... Crowds arrived, and I shall never forget the grand sight. My humble pen can never describe it. I was a little annoyed with Carrie, who kept saying: 'Isn't it a pity we don't know anybody?'

Once she quite lost her head. I saw someone who looked like Franching, from Peckham, and was moving towards him when she seized me by the coat-tails, and said, quite loudly: 'Don't leave me,' which caused an elderly gentleman, in a court-suit, and a chain round him, and two ladies, to burst out laughing. There was an immense crowd in the supper-room, and, my stars! it was splendid supper – any amount of champagne.

Carrie made a most hearty supper, for which I was pleased; for I sometimes think she is not strong. There was scarcely a dish she did not taste. I was so thirsty, I could not eat much. Receiving a sharp slap on the shoulder, I turned, and, to my amazement, saw Farmerson, our ironmonger. He said, in the most familiar way: 'This is better than Brickfield Terrace, eh?' I simply looked at him, and said coolly: 'I never expected to see you here.' He said, with a loud, coarse laugh: 'I like that – if *you*, why not *me*?' I replied 'Certainly.' I wish I could have thought of something better to say. He said: 'Can I get your good lady anything?' Carrie said: 'No, I thank you,' for which I was pleased. I said, by way of reproof to him: 'You never sent to-day to paint the bath as I requested.' Farmerson said: 'Pardon me, Mr Pooter, no shop when we're in company, please.'

> GEORGE AND WEEDON GROSSMITH
> *The Diary of a Nobody*, 1892

James Whistler was told that the committee of an international art competition had awarded him its Gold Medal. However, the fact that they qualified it by making it the Gold Medal, Second Class, Whistler rightly perceived as a snub. The artist wrote back in the following terms:

'Pray convey my sentiments of tempered and respectful joy to the gentlemen of the committee, and my complete appreciation of the second-class compliment paid to me.'

William Taft, President of the United States from 1909 to 1913, was a man of ample girth. At an official dinner he was teased about his size by Chauncey Depew:

'I hope, if it's a girl, Mr Taft will name it for his charming wife,' laughed Depew with a meaningful look at Taft's large stomach.

'Of course, if it's a girl, I shall name it for my lovely helpmate of many years,' replied Taft. 'If it's a boy, I shall claim the father's prerogative and call it William Taft Junior. But if, as I suspect, it is merely a bag of wind, I shall call it Chauncey Depew.'

Here is a tale of snub and counter-snub involving two gifted but temperamental performers; the American diseuse and monologist Ruth Draper and the English actress Irene Vanbrugh. Both ladies were at a glittering occasion and elegantly attired but Miss Vanbrugh was sporting a particularly arresting pair of elbow-length white kid gloves. Feeling rather put out Miss Draper indicated Irene Vanbrugh's prized gloves and said contemptuously:

'Skin of a beast.'

'Oh, what do you wear?' asked Miss Vanbrugh.

'Why, silk, of course,' replied Miss Draper.

'Entrails of a worm,' remarked Miss Vanbrugh, gliding triumphantly away.

Playwright Clare Boothe Luce and Dorothy Parker, both known for their ready wit, arrived simultaneously at a smart society party.

'Age before beauty,' hissed Miss Luce, making way for Miss Parker.

'Pearls before swine,' countered Miss Parker striding confidently ahead.

Two legendary exchanges involve Winston Churchill and women MPs.

'Winston, you're drunk,' said Bessie Braddock, as Churchill emerged from an indulgent dinner in the Members' Dining Room.

'And Bessie, you are ugly,' countered Churchill, 'but tomorrow morning *I* shall be sober.'

Churchill had a long-standing aversion to Lady Astor, an American by birth, the first woman to take up her seat in the House of Commons and a proselytizing teetotaller. Lady Astor had an equal aversion to Sir Winston. During one of their many acerbic confrontations Lady Astor informed Sir Winston:

'If you were my husband I would put poison in your coffee.'

'Madam,' he replied gravely, 'if you were my wife, I would drink it.'

Actress Ina Claire was briefly married to John Gilbert the romantic star of Hollywood's silent movie era. During a press call she was asked:

'How does it feel to be married to a celebrity?'

'Why not ask my husband?' replied Miss Claire.

Bernard Shaw found a copy of his plays in a second-hand bookshop and was understandably offended to find that the inside cover carried a personal inscription from himself to a friend. In response to the implied snub he bought the book, wrote 'With the renewed compliments of Bernard Shaw,' underneath the original inscription, and sent it back to his friend without a covering note.

Noel Coward was known as the Master, not least for his spontaneous wit. During a performance of one of Coward's plays the broadcaster Gilbert Harding had promptly fallen asleep and had snored loudly throughout. Meeting him after the show Harding apologized profusely to Coward for his undoubtedly insulting behaviour.

'No need to apologize, my dear fellow,' replied Coward graciously. 'After all, I have never bored you one half as much as you have bored me.'

Coward did not always have the last word. Encountering Pulitzer prize-winning writer Edna Ferber dressed in a suit almost identical with his own, he observed:

'Edna, you look almost like a man.'

'So do you,' came the swift riposte.

At a smart reception a lady clearly conscious of her superior social status approached the Canadian actress, Beatrice Lillie. 'What beautiful pearls, Miss Lillie. Are they real?' she cooed.

'Of course,' Miss Lillie replied.

Unconvinced the woman arrogantly took hold of the long string of pearls and tested one between her teeth. 'They're not real,' she crowed, 'they're cultured.'

'And how would you know, Duchess, with your false teeth?' retorted the actress.

Dorothy Parker was accosted by a so-called friend at a cocktail party who commented:

'Don't you think that dress is a little young on you, darling?'

'Perhaps, dear,' replied the unflappable Mrs Parker. 'Yours looks lovely on you, but then it always does.'

While Australian Prime Minister Robert Menzies was campaigning a disgruntled voter called out:

'I wouldn't vote for you if you were the Archangel Gabriel himself.'

'If I were the Archangel Gabriel,' riposted Menzies, '*you* wouldn't be in my constituency.'

Sir Thomas Beecham was travelling in a No Smoking compartment of a train, in which the only other passenger, an elegantly dressed woman, lit up a cigarette.

'I'm sure you will not mind if I smoke,' she said graciously.

'Not at all. I'm sure you will not mind if I am sick,' rejoined Beecham, equally graciously …

'You do not realize,' she countered, 'that I am one of the directors' wives.'

'Madam, were you the director's only wife, I should still be sick,' said Beecham.

To an aspiring author who had hoped for praise Dr Johnson wrote:

'Your manuscript is both good and original; but the part that is good is not original, and the part that is original is not good.'

Somerset Maugham, who had been invited on to the set of *Doctor Jekyll and Mr Hyde*, watched Spencer Tracy for several takes before remarking to his companion: 'Which one is he playing now?'

The flamboyant and malicious American theatre critic Alexander Woollcott was discussing the possibility of a revival of *Macbeth* on Broadway. Knowing she aspired to the role Woollcott turned to the actress Peggy Wood and said:

'I don't think you would make a very good Lady Macbeth, do you Peggy?'

'No, Alec,' she agreed, 'but you would.'

On one occasion while accompanied by fellow journalist and wit Franklin Pierce Adams, Woollcott was approached by an admirer and asked to sign a first edition of his book *Shouts and Murmurs*.

'Ah, what is so rare as a Woollcott first edition?' he

murmured approvingly to his admirer as he granted the request.

'A Woollcott second edition,' responded Adams.

In 1926 American humorist Robert Benchley was at the first night of *The Squall*. A feature of the play was the frequent use of a sort of pidgin English dialogue. Eventually Benchley had had enough. When a young gypsy announced:

'Me Nubi. Nubi good girl. Me stay.'

Benchley capped it with:

'Me Bobby. Bobby bad boy. Me go.' Upon which he left the auditorium.

The seventeenth-century divine Dr Robert South found himself in the unenviable position of preaching to the secular court of Charles II. It was not unknown for the king and his courtiers to nod off during a good sermon, but Dr South could not overlook this indelicate want of concentration. Unable to call the king to attention he targeted a man close by, departing from his chosen text with the words:

'Lord Lauderdale, let me entreat you, rouse yourself. You snore so loud you will wake the king.'

The Lord Sandwich, who was first Lord of the Admiralty in 1771, was, as the world said, very profligate, and without religious principles. Dr Scott, of Simonbourn, dined at his table, and as report stated, was about to say grace before dinner, when Lord Sandwich said:

'Stay, doctor, I have a chaplain of my own who is coming into the room,' and immediately a monkey was introduced dressed in canonicals. Scott then apologized for having obtruded his services, assuring Lord Sandwich that he did not know his lordship had a relation in orders.

LORD ELDON

George Canning, who was briefly Prime Minister in 1827, was asked by a vicar how he had enjoyed his sermon.

'You were brief ...' Canning began.

'Ah, yes,' interrupted the vicar, 'I like to avoid being tedious.'

'... But you were tedious,' continued Canning.

Richard Whately, Archbishop of Dublin in the early nineteenth century, was approached by an earnest young clergyman:

'I hope your Grace will excuse my preaching next Sunday.'

'Certainly.'

Sunday came, and the Archbishop said to him:

'Well, Mr – what became of you? We expected you to preach today?'

'Oh, your Grace said he would excuse my preaching today.'

'Exactly,' responded the Archbishop, 'but I did not say I would excuse you *from* preaching.'

He [Whately] lived upon easy terms with the young men about the viceregal court, and one of them, a young nobleman who was aide-de-camp to the Lord Lieutenant, made a little mistake in assuming that a scoff at the Roman Catholic bishops would be acceptable:

'My Lord Archbishop,' said the aide-de-camp, 'do

you know what is the difference between a Roman Catholic bishop and a donkey?'

'No,' said the archbishop.

'The one has a cross on his breast and the other on his back,' said the aide-de-camp.

'Ha!' said the archbishop, 'do you know the difference between an aide-de-camp and a donkey?'

'No,' said the aide-de-camp.

'Neither do I,' said the archbishop.

> HENRY TAYLOR
> *Autobiography*, 1885

A Boston citizen, whose morals left a great deal to be desired, nevertheless maintained an outward show of hypocritical and somewhat censorious piety.

'Before I die it is my greatest wish to visit the Holy Land and recite the Ten Commandments on the summit of Mount Sinai,' he confided to Mark Twain.

'Is that so?' said Twain. 'Why not just stay right here in Boston and try to keep them?'

At the outbreak of the American Civil War Abraham Lincoln was discussing the sad turn of events with a clergyman after church service.

'Let us have faith, Mr President, that the Lord is on our side in this great struggle,' said the man.

'I am not at all concerned about that, for I know the Lord is always on the side of right,' replied the President, 'but it is my constant anxiety and prayer that this nation may be on the Lord's side.'

As Tolstoy lay dying his friends, with the best of intentions, tried to persuade him to reconcile himself with the Orthodox Church. Tolstoy poured cold water on their well-meaning protestations with the observation:

'Even in the valley of the shadow of death two and two do not make six.'

The Archbishop of Canterbury, Cosmo Gordon Lang, had commissioned a portrait of himself to mark his accession to his high office in 1928. When the Bishop of Durham, Hensley Henson, called on him the Archbishop showed him the new painting and asked his opinion of it. Unwilling to commit himself Henson asked the Archbishop for his own opinion.

'I fear it portrays me as proud, arrogant and worldly,' said Lang.

'And to which of these attributes does your Grace take exception?' asked Henson.

Ever since his days at Blundells Frederick Temple had enjoyed community singing, and often turning his collar round he never missed the chance to join in a rousing hymn or carol during his five years as Archbishop of Canterbury. On one of his visits around the country he was passing a church when the sound of lusty singing lured him inside. Squeezing into a space in a pew he picked up a hymn book and joined in. After he had sung no more than a couple of verses, the man standing next to him nudged him in the side and said under his breath:

'Dry up mister. You're spoiling the show.'
  KENNETH WILLIAMS
  Acid Drops, 1980

Hearing that Bernard Shaw had a foolproof method of brewing coffee an unassuming country parson wrote and asked for instructions. Shaw sent off the reply but added a rather testy postscript saying that he hoped this was not simply an underhand way of obtaining his autograph. Back came a thank-you note together with Shaw's signature, neatly cut out of his letter. Added to the thanks was the clergyman's own postscript:

'I wrote in good faith, so allow me to return what it is obvious you infinitely prize, but which is of no value to me, your autograph.'

In the early weeks of 1994 casting director Noel Davis was 'church-tasting' and attended a service at St Peter's, Eaton Square. The church prides itself on its musical tradition and during a rather extended Gloria in the style of Benjamin Britten, Davis found himself glancing surreptitiously at his watch. This did not go unnoticed by the officiating clergyman who had clearly 'clocked' the moment of inattention.

After the service the vicar was standing at the west door to greet the emerging congregation. As they shook hands he remarked to Davis:

'I hope you catch your train.' Which drew the surprised response:

'I'm not catching a train, I'm having lunch at the Garrick.'

'Well,' replied the vicar smoothly, 'that's important too.'

Doctor Johnson did not suffer fools gladly and had no fear of hurting feelings. He upbraided an acquaintance for the pointless and demeaning way in which he earned a living so that the man was stung to retaliate:

'Well, Doctor, I have to live.'

'I do not see the least necessity for that,' was the uncompromising reply.

Johnson himself scraped a precarious living from his various journalistic and literary works. While his wife was alive this was a source of constant anxiety, but after her death Johnson found himself indifferent to money. In 1755 his *Dictionary of the English Language* appeared. This prompted Lord Chesterfield to offer him his patronage. Johnson's letter of refusal has become famous:

'The notice which you have been pleased to take of my labours, had it been early, had been kind; but it has been delayed till I am indifferent, and cannot enjoy it; till I am solitary, and cannot impart it; till I am known, and do not want it.'

To all letters soliciting 'his subscription' to anything, Lord Erskine, the Prince Regent's chancellor, had a regular form of reply, viz:

'Sir, I feel very much honoured by your application to me, and I beg to subscribe,' – here the reader had to turn over the leaf – 'myself your very obedient servant, etc.'
    SAMUEL ROGERS
    Rogers's Table-Talk and Porsoniana, 1856

Essayist Joseph Addison relished the stimulating arguments he enjoyed with a friend on a wide range of topics. There came a time when the friend was in need of money, which Addison readily loaned him. However this took its toll on their friendship. The friend became fearful of disagreeing with Addison and echoed everything he said. Eventually Addison could stand this dispiriting docility no longer. Turning on his friend he declared:

'Either contradict me, sir, or pay me my money.'

John Jacob Astor, who was the richest man in America when he died in 1848, never lost his pleasure in a sharp deal. A typical story told of him concerns a plot of real estate near Wall Street which he sold for $8,000. The buyer had got himself something of a bargain, and could not resist saying so. Thinking he had outsmarted Astor he allowed himself the pleasure of remarking that in only a few years the land would have increased in value by at least 50%.

'In a few years this lot will be worth twelve thousand dollars.'

'You're right,' said Astor unperturbed. 'But with your eight thousand I intend to buy eighty lots above Canal Street, and by the time your lot is worth twelve thousand dollars, my eighty lots will be worth eighty thousand dollars.'

Douglas Jerrold, playwright and regular contributor to *Punch*, was approached by a man asking for financial assistance for a mutual friend. This was not the first time such an approach had been made and Jerrold was not as willing as on previous occasions.

'How much does he want?' he inquired.

'A four and two noughts will clear the debt,' replied the other.

'Put me down for one of the noughts,' said Jerrold.

William Vanderbilt, son of the founder of the Vanderbilt fortune and a railroad magnate himself, was approached by a pushy newspaper reporter. The man demanded to know the answer to several questions relating to the company, claiming his investigations were 'in the public interest'.

'Public be damned,' barked Vanderbilt. '*I* am working for my stockholders.'

Cornelius Vanderbilt, President of the New York Central Railroad, received a letter from George Westinghouse, an unknown engineer who claimed to have devised an automatic air brake. Vanderbilt turned him down arbitrarily, returning his letter with the following message written on it:

'I have no time to waste on fools. Cornelius Vanderbilt.'

In a relatively short period Westinghouse had achieved enormous success with the invention, which he developed with the Pennsylvania Railroad. Vanderbilt then wrote to him, asking to meet him. Back came the reply, written on the bottom of Vanderbilt's own letter:

'I have no time to waste on fools. George Westinghouse.'

When Sir Herbert Beerbohm Tree acquired His Majesty's Theatre he was determined to build up the most attractive company available. He invited one very popular actor, with a strong personal following, to join him in his dressing room before a performance. As Beerbohm Tree began to apply his elaborate make-up the two men prepared to discuss terms.

'What salary are you looking for?' asked Tree.

The actor, who had a strong sense of his own worth, named a price. Without glancing away from the mirror Tree replied:

'Please don't slam the door when you leave.'

To a person who wants to borrow Money without any claim but assurance.

Hill Side, Blackheath,
(Date in full ——)

Sir,

While I was out of town I find you did me the honour of inquiring two or three times for me; and among my letters I found one from you desiring the loan of £10. You must certainly have mistaken me or yourself very much to think we were sufficiently intimate to warrant such a request. Were I to answer the demand of every new acquaintance, I should soon want power to oblige my old friends, and even to serve himself. Surely a gentleman of your merit cannot be so little beloved as to be forced to seek new acquaintances, and to have no better friend than one of yesterday. Be this as it may, it does not at all suit my convenience to comply with your request, and therefore I must beg you to excuse

Yours obediently,

Charles Grey

(Name and Address)

> *Beeton's Complete Letter-Writer for Ladies and Gentlemen*

A cabman complained to Lord Rothschild that the tip he had just given him was only half what had been given to him a few days earlier by Lord Rothschild's own son. Declining to augment the sum Lord Rothschild explained:

'You see, my son has a millionaire for a father. I do not.'

Samuel Goldwyn, the Hollywood movie mogul, was anxious to acquire the screen rights to the plays of Bernard Shaw. Hoping to flatter Shaw into naming a low price he wrote:

'Think of the millions of people who would get to see your plays who would otherwise never have the chance. Think of the contribution to art.' To which Shaw sent the reply:

'The trouble is, Mr Goldwyn, that you think of nothing but art, and I think of nothing but money.'

Dramatist Lillian Hellman was among a number of women sent a survey by *Harper's Magazine.* This survey had originally been intended for men and included the question:

'During which activity, situation, moment or moments do you feel most masculine?' Hellman's reply went straight to the point:

'It makes me feel masculine to tell you that I do not answer questions like this without being paid to answer them.'

As a young man James Joyce, whose father was a tax inspector, applied for a job in a bank and felt fairly confident as he answered the bank manager's questions.

'Do you smoke?'

'No.'

'Drink?'

'No.'

'Run around with girls?'

'No.'

'Then I'm afraid we can't use you. You'd probably rob the bank.'

Henry Labouchère was a Liberal MP in the mid-nineteenth century. He began his career in the diplomatic service. While he was attaché to the Russian court at St Petersburg a man presented himself and demanded to be taken immediately to the ambassador.

'Pray take a chair while I discover whether the ambassador can see you,' said Labouchère.

This enraged the visitor who insisted that his rank and eminence entitled him to an immediate interview.

'Do you know who you are talking to, young man?' he barked and proceeded to reel off an exhaustive list of his titles, ranks and awards.

'In that case,' said Labouchère politely, 'please take two chairs.'

Lord Curzon, that most superior person, was appointed Viceroy of India in 1898 and was later Foreign Secretary. He travelled extensively in the Far East over a period of years. On a fact-finding visit to Japan he was disconcerted to come across a group of women bathing naked in a pool by the roadside. Asking his interpreter to stop their carriage he watched amazed for a while and then asked the man whether it was not considered indecent in Japan for people to appear naked in public.

'No,' replied the man, 'but it *is* regarded as indecent to watch them.'

While travelling in France Mark Twain stayed with Paul Bourget, the French poet and novelist. Referring patronizingly to the relatively short history of the United States as an independent country Bourget observed:

'Life can never be entirely dull for an American. When he has nothing else to do he can always spend a few years trying to discover who his grandfather was.'

32

'Very true,' returned Twain, 'but a Frenchman too has an interesting task for his idle moments; he can spend a little time trying to find out who his father was.'

Arthur Balfour visited the United States and was given a conducted tour of New York. As part of the tour he was taken to see the city's newest and tallest skyscraper. 'Remarkable, remarkable,' acknowledged Balfour as he was plied with information about its height, its method of construction, the short time it had tken to complete, the number of men it had taken to build it and how much it cost. Finally it was explained to him that new methods of construction meant the skyscraper would stand for a thousand years.

'Dear, dear me, what a great pity,' he murmured.

Between the wars Hitler travelled to Rome on a goodwill visit to Mussolini. Hermann Goering, Hitler's right-hand man, accompanied him. As Goering and his bodyguards forced their way through the crowds a tall aristocratic-looking man stood his ground, demanding an apology for being pushed and shoved.

'I am Hermann Goering,' asserted the German officer.

'As an excuse that is inadequate,' said the Roman, 'but as an explanation it is quite sufficient.'

Peter [Page] told us a yarn which he protested was true. He was on a cruise, and the boat stopped at a tiny islet in the Marquesas, visited every five years or so. Going ashore he encountered on the beach a youth wearing nothing but a pair of soiled shorts. Peter told him in his best French all about the Atlantic flights of Hughes and Corrigan.

'I suppose,' he added, 'in view of your isolation, you

must find it a great treat to talk to anybody?' The young man, who had done nothing but stare, said in broad cockney:

'I don't know wot you're talking abaht. I'm a steward on B deck.'

JAMES AGATE
A Shorter Ego, 1946

While staying in New York Sir Thomas Beecham received a phone call from a man with a strong Southern accent:

'Is thaat Sah Thaamas Beech'm?'

'It is.'

'This here's thah President of thah Inglish speakin' Yuhnion.'

'I beg your pardon?'

The message was repeated.

'I simply don't believe it,' said Sir Thomas crisply and replaced the receiver.

At an international conference in Geneva in 1956 the then Foreign Secretary, Harold Macmillan, asked Lord Gladwyn to lend some of the magnificent silver from the British Embassy in Paris, so that he could welcome his fellow ministers in style. Sitting next to dour Molotov at Macmillan's dinner party, Gladwyn asked him whether he did not admire the silver plate, the huge salvers along which the wall and the great candelabra by which the room was lit.

'In Moscow,' Molotov replied, 'we have *electric* light.'

KENNETH ROSE
Sunday Telegraph, 16 November 1986

At the height of the 'Cold War' Harold Macmillan, by now elevated to Prime Minister, was invited to address the Security Council of the United Nations. Nikita Khrushchev, the Soviet Prime Minister, was present at the occasion. He disagreed violently with the content of Macmillan's speech and chose to display his disapproval by removing one of his shoes and banging it furiously on the table. Unperturbed Macmillan turned good-humouredly to the interpreters and said:

'I wonder if I might have a translation?'

While he was Lord Chancellor Francis Bacon presided over the appeal of a man called Hogg. Hogg appealed to the Lord Chancellor on the grounds of kinship as Hogg must be kin to Bacon.

'Not until it has been hung,' replied Bacon tartly.

An attorney in Dublin having died exceedingly poor, a shilling subscription was set on foot to pay the expenses of his burial. Most of the attorneys and barristers having subscribed, one of them applied to Toler, afterwards Lord Chief Justice Norbury, expressing his hope that he would also subscribe his shilling.

'Only a shilling,' said Toler, 'only a shilling to bury an attorney? Here is a guinea; go and bury one and twenty of them.'

LORD ELDON

Sir Fletcher Norton was a lawyer with an unenviable reputation for rudeness, both in court and in private life. On one occasion he was appearing in a case about the ownership of land and arguing an obscure point of law over who had first claim to several manors.

'My lord,' he said to Lord Mansfield, the presiding judge, 'I think I can illustrate this point in an instance in my own person. I myself have two little manors.'

'We all know it, Sir Fletcher,' affirmed the judge.

Lord Erskine's humour was chiefly illustrated by his cross-examination of witnesses ... Experience had probably shown him that a cause was more often served by upsetting the gravity of a jury than combating the opinions of his opponents. A witness who had baffled his examination was suddenly asked by him:

'You were born and bred in Manchester, I believe?'

'I was,' answered the witness pompously.

'I knew it,' said Erskine, 'from the absurd cut of your neckcloth.'

WILLIAM CLARK RUSSELL
The Book of Table-Talk, 1834

Lord Chief Justice Ellenborough, who was appointed Governor-General of India in 1841, was hearing an interminable case in which the defence counsel spoke with scarcely a pause from the beginning of the day until four o'clock. At this point the barrister, observing the time, asked his lordship when it would be the court's pleasure to hear the rest of his argument on behalf of his client.

'We are bound to hear you, sir,' replied Ellenborough, 'and shall do so again on Friday; but pleasure has long been out of the question.'

Appearing before Lord Clare, a barrister tried to make an impact by bringing a live eagle as evidence into the court-room. Anxious to impress he proceeded to develop a long and elaborate metaphor relating the bird and the case. So complicated was his train of thought that eventually the barrister, like everyone else in the court, lost the thread of what he was trying to illustrate. His confusion was cut short by Lord Clare who observed:

'The next time, sir, that you bring an eagle into court, I recommend that you clip its wings.'

F.E. Smith was questioning a witness:

'So what you are, in fact, saying, is that you were as drunk as a judge?'

At this point the judge leaned forward and intervened:

'I think you will find, Mr Smith, that the expression is "as drunk as a lord." '

F.E. Smith's response was unhesitating:

'As your lordship pleases.'

When F.E. Smith, opening a case before Mr Justice Ridley, rose to address the jury, the judge most injudiciously observed:

'Well, Mr Smith, I have read the pleadings and I do not think much of your case.' Smith replied quickly:

'Indeed, I am sorry to hear that, m'Lud, but your lordship will find that the more you hear of it, the more it will grow on you.'

> 2ND LORD BIRKENHEAD
> *Life of Lord Birkenhead*, 1933

The libel jury in the *EastEnders* 'sex romp' case were entertained yesterday to a clash between two leading barristers ...

Speaking of Mr Carman, counsel for the *Sun* ... Mr Beloff told the jury that when it came to exciting prejudice and evoking sympathy they had heard a 'past

and present master' of the art. 'Mr Carman's final speech in a libel action is always a source of entertainment – especially if you hear it for the first time.'
The Times, 19 January 1994

Dr Johnson was being pursued by a lady who had written a tragedy and was anxious for his opinion of it. Johnson tried many times to extricate himself from this task without unkindness. The lady was unrelenting. Eventually Johnson told her that it would be best if she were to read it through carefully herself, in which case she would identify the faults which he would discover were he to read it.

'But sir,' she replied, 'I have no time, I have already so many irons in the fire.'

'Why then, madam,' he rejoined, 'the best thing I can advise you to do is to put your tragedy in the fire along with your irons.'

Dr Bentley's son reading a novel, the doctor said:
  'Why read a book which you cannot quote?'
    HORACE WALPOLE
    Walpoliana

Antoine de Rivarol, the eighteenth-century French writer and pamphleteer, was chiefly renowned for his sarcasm. An unwary aspiring poet cornered de Rivarol and asked him to give an honest assessment of a couplet he had penned. De Rivarol read it through several times with great ceremony, then gave his opinion:
  'Very nice, but it does have its *longueurs*.'

Voltaire and Rousseau were two of France's greatest literary figures. They are buried alongside one another in the Pantheon in Paris. It is uncertain what Voltaire would have made of this proximity since on the publication of Rousseau's ode *To Posterity*, Voltaire remarked:

'This poem will not reach its destination.'

The poet Fontenelle was critical of Voltaire's much-acclaimed poem, *Oedipe*, saying that he found certain verses 'too strong and full of fire.' To which Voltaire replied:

'To correct this tendency I shall read your *Pastorales*'.

Not all snubs are intentional. The Hanoverian men were not renowned, on the whole, for their intellectual capacities, so the great historian, Edward Gibbon, was delighted when the Duke of Gloucester showed an interest in his work. He presented him with an inscribed copy of the first volume of his *Decline and Fall of the Roman Empire*. On publication of the second volume he again visited the Duke with a copy. The Duke greeted him with enthusiasm, took the book, placed it on a table unopened and said heartily:

'Another damn'd thick, square book! Always scribble, scribble, scribble, eh, Mr Gibbon?'

Talleyrand, the one-time bishop, revolutionary, right-hand man of Napoleon and later a conspirator in his overthrow, was a profoundly cynical man. One of his many verbal sparring partners was the novelist Mme de Stael. In 1802 she published the novel *Delphine*, whose heroine was assumed to be based on Mme de Stael herself. Another character, an elderly matron, was commonly believed to be based on Talleyrand. Meeting Mme de Stael Talleyrand neatly turned this presumed insult with the remark:

'They tell me we are both of us depicted in your novel, Madame, and both of us in the disguise of women.'
Memoirs of Prince Talleyrand

A well-known author exclaimed:

'During my life I have been guilty of only one mistake.'

Talleyrand said:

'When will it end?'
WILLIAM CLARK RUSSELL
The Book of Table-Talk, 1834

Charles Lamb, the essayist and author, with his sister, of *Tales from Shakespeare*, was talking of literature with his friend, the poet Wordsworth.

'I believe I could write like Shakespeare if I had mind to it,' averred Wordsworth.

'Yes,' agreed Lamb, 'nothing wanting but the mind.'

On another occasion Wordsworth was having a conversation with Sir Walter Scott in which he declared:

'I have the greatest contempt for Aristotle.'

'But not, I take it,' answered Scott, 'that contempt which familiarity breeds.'

Mr [Samuel] Rogers told me that when *Pleasures of Memory* was first published, one of those busy gentlemen who are vain of knowing everybody came up to him at a party and said:

'Lady —— is dying to be introduced to the author of the *Pleasures of Memory*.'

'Pray let her live,' said Rogers, and with difficulty they made their way through the crowd to the lady.

'Mr Rogers, madam, author of *Pleasures of Memory*.'

'Pleasures of *what*?'

'I felt for my friend,' said Rogers.

> C.R. LESLIE
> *Autobiographical Recollections*, 1860

In 1836 Charlotte Brontë wrote to Robert Southey asking whether he thought she could earn her living as a writer. The poet replied with 'a dose of cooling admonition':

'Literature cannot be the business of a woman's life, and it ought not to be. The more she is engaged in her proper duties, the less leisure she will have for it, even as an accomplishment and recreation. To those duties you have not yet been called, and when you are, you will be less eager for celebrity.'

William Thackeray was on a lecture tour of the United States. In St Louis he dined in a hotel where he heard himself referred to by two Irish waiters:

'Do you know who that is?'

'No.'

'That is the celebrated Thacker.'

'What's *he* done?'

'D——d if *I* know.'

Although gratified by the success of her books and the financial security they brought her, Louisa May Alcott did not always enjoy the attention she attracted. At a suffragette rally in Syracuse she was approached by an overpowering admirer:

'If you ever come to Oshkosh your feet will not be allowed to touch the ground; you will be borne in the arms of the people. Will you come?'

'Never,' replied Miss Alcott firmly.

The historian Oscar Browning liked to claim the friendship of well-known literary figures. He therefore made a visit to the Isle of Wight expressly to meet Tennyson. Accosting the Poet Laureate he grasped him firmly, if unexpectedly, by the hand and declared:

'I'm Browning.'

Tennyson, for whom the poet of that name was the only Browning who mattered, withdrew his hand, declared equally firmly:

'No, you're not,' and made his escape.

The French salonnière Euphrasie Aubernon ran her salon with a rod of iron, setting topics for discussion and ringing a bell to bring her guests to order. On the whole the guests submitted in a docile fashion. However on one occasion Geneviève Halévy Strauss arrived late. Mme Aubernon made her displeasure apparent by leaving her no time to settle down before ringing the handbell and announcing:

'Our topic for today is adultery. Mme Strauss may we hear your thoughts?'

'Forgive me,' replied Mme Strauss, 'I'm afraid I have only come prepared for incest.'

Edith Wharton made her first attempt at a novel when she was only eleven years old. Proudly she showed her work to her mother. The novel began promisingly:

'Oh, how do you do, Mrs Brown?' said Mrs Tompkins. 'If only I had known you were going to call I should have tidied up the drawing-room.'

Mrs Wharton's only comment was:

'Drawing-rooms are always tidy.'

Robert Frost, much of whose work celebrates the New England landscape, was enjoying postprandial coffee on the veranda with his fellow dinner guests. It was a summer evening and there was a spectacular late sunset.

'Isn't the sunset wonderful, Mr Frost?' enthused a young woman moving over to join him.

'I never discuss business after dinner,' he said shortly.

James Barrie's *Peter Pan* brought him great renown but he always reacted badly when people tried to accost him at home. A reporter was about to ring his doorbell just as Barrie arrived home.

'Sir James Barrie I presume?' he began.

'You do,' said Barrie, going inside and slamming the door.

Bernard Shaw never shrank from criticizing the talents and opinions of others. His criticism of G.K. Chesterton's ideas about the economy appeared prominently in print. Surprisingly Chesterton did not retaliate. This annoyed his friend, Hilaire Belloc, who asked why he remained silent. Chesterton explained:

'My dear Belloc, I *have* answered him. To a man of Shaw's wit, silence is the one unbearable repartee.'

Dame Edith Evans was told that Nancy Mitford had borrowed a friend's house in the South of France in order to 'finish a book'. 'Oh really?' she inquired, 'What is she reading?'

James Joyce was accosted by an enthusiastic admirer: 'May I kiss the hand that wrote *Ulysses*?'

James Joyce: 'You may not. It did other things too.'

Gertrude Stein, the American novelist, based her writing style on abstract painting, with some rather strange results, not least a tendency to repeat all her phrases many times. Entering into the spirit of experimental literature a publisher sent her the following letter of rejection:

'I am only one, only one, only one. Only one life to live, only sixty minutes in one hour. Only one pair of eyes. Only one brain, only one being. Being only one, having only one pair of eyes, having only one time, having only one life, I cannot read your manuscript three or four times. Not even one time. Only one look, only one look is enough. Hardly one copy would sell here. Hardly one. Hardly one.'

A conference on the art of writing was arranged at Columbia University. Among the eminent novelists booked to address the aspiring wordsmiths was Sinclair Lewis. At the time advertised Lewis rose, stood at the lectern and began:

'Which of you here is really serious about being a writer?'

There was a great show of hands as the audience eagerly awaited enlightenment.

'Then why the hell aren't you back at home writing?' responded Lewis and promptly sat down again.

Sunday 20 August 1939

At dinner Leo said:

'Times have changed, James, and you with them.

When I first knew you in 1921 your motto was "In the beginning was the word." Now it appears to be "In the end is the cheque." '
JAMES AGATE
A Shorter Ego, 1946

John Dryden's marriage was not always congenial to him, and he often took refuge in his work.

'Lord, Mr Dryden, how can you always be poring over those musty books?' complained Lady Elizabeth. 'I wish I were a book, and then I should have more of your company.'

'Pray, my dear,' he replied, 'if you do become a book, let it be an almanack, for then I may change you every year.'

The 6th Duke of Somerset was known as 'The Proud Duke'. He added greatly to the family name and fortune by marrying Elizabeth Percy, an heiress to the fortune of the Dukes of Northumberland. After her death in 1722 he married, less advantageously, a daughter of the Earl of Nottingham. This lady made the mistake of prejudicing her husband's ducal dignity by tapping his arm with her fan to attract his attention. Turning on her he announced:

'Madam, my first wife never took such a liberty and *she* was a Percy.'

Olivia: Dear me! I wish this journey were over. No news of Jarvis yet? I believe the old peevish creature delays purely to vex me.

Garnet: Why, to be sure, madam. I did hear him say, a little snubbing before marriage would teach you to bear it better afterwards.

OLIVER GOLDSMITH
The Good Natured Man, 1768

A French gentleman, being married a second time, was often lamenting his first wife before his second, who one day said to him:

'I assure you, sir, no one regrets her more than I.'

HORACE WALPOLE

'And all your notes,' said Dorothea, whose heart had already burned within her on this subject so that now she could not help speaking with her tongue. 'All those rows of volumes – will you not now do what you used to speak of? – will you not make up your mind what part of them you will use, and begin to write the book which will make your vast knowledge useful to the world? I will write to your dictation, or I will copy and extract what you tell me: I can be of no other use.' Dorothea, in a most unaccountable, darkly-feminine manner, ended with a slight sob and eyes full of tears.

The excessive feeling manifested would alone have been highly disturbing to Mr Casaubon, but there were other reasons why Dorothea's words were among the most cutting and irritating to him that she could have been impelled to use ... In Mr Casaubon's ear, Dorothea's voice gave loud emphatic iteration to those muffled suggestions of consciousness which it was possible to explain as mere fancy, the illusion of exaggerated sensitiveness: always when such suggestions are unmistakably repeated from without, they are resisted as cruel and unjust ... For the first time since Dorothea had known him Mr Casaubon's face had a quick angry flush upon it.

'My love,' he said, with irritation reined in by propriety, 'you may rely upon me for knowing the times and the seasons, adapted to the different stages of a work which is not to be measured by the facile conjectures of ignorant onlookers. It had been easy for me to gain a temporary effect by a mirage of baseless opinion; but it was ever the trial of the scrupulous explorer to be saluted with the impatient scorn of chatterers who attempt only the smallest achievements, being indeed equipped for no other. And it were well if all such could be admonished to discriminate judgments of which the true subject-matter lies entirely beyond their reach, from those of which the elements may be compassed by a narrow and superficial survey.'

GEORGE ELIOT
Middlemarch, 1871–2

John Abernethy was an eminent surgeon at the beginning of the nineteenth century. He was as well known for his short temper as for his great skill.

Mrs J—— consulted him respecting a nervous disorder, the minutiae of which appeared so fantastic that Mr A. interrupted their frivolous detail by holding out his hand for the fee. A one-pound note and a shilling were placed upon it; upon which he returned the latter to the fair patient, with the angry exclamation:

'There, Ma'am! go and buy a skipping rope; that is all you want.'

F. WINSLOW
Physic and Physicians

The German poet Otto Hartleben consulted a doctor when he began to feel unwell. The doctor examined him thoroughly and offered his advice: Hartleben should give up smoking and drinking. As the poet made for the door the doctor called out:

'The fee for my advice is three marks.'

'I'm not taking your advice,' replied Hartleben and disappeared out of the door.

During the American Civil War Abraham Lincoln was constantly irritated by the lethargy of one of his generals, George B. McLellan, and eventually dismissed him. Having received a typically procrastinating dispatch from McLellan Lincoln sent the following response:

'Major-General McLellan, I have just read your dispatch about sore-tongued and fatigued horses. Will you pardon me for asking what the horses of your army have done since the battle of Antietam that fatigues anything?'

Henry Ward Beecher was an anti-slavery campaigner who travelled to England during the American Civil War to gain support for the Northern cause. While addressing a crowd in Manchester he was heckled.

'Why didn't you whip the Confederates in sixty days as you said you would?'

'Because we found we had Americans to fight this time, not Englishmen,' Beecher shouted back.

During the Boer War a statement was made in the House of Commons by the Secretary of State for War in which he detailed the number of horses and mules which had been sent out to South Africa. Reflecting the contempt felt by many people for the generals running the campaign Irish Nationalist MP Timothy Healy asked:

'And can the right honourable gentleman tell me how many asses have been sent?'

Field-Marshall Earl Wavell's military achievements included being Commander-in-Chief of British forces in the Middle East, and Supreme Commander of allied forces in the Southwest Pacific, before his appointment as Viceroy of India in 1943. A former pupil at Winchester he had to be content with the following entry in the school magazine:

'Wavell, A.P. Had a good war.'

Dr Johnson had spent a disagreeable evening trapped into listening to his hostess play the harpsichord. Johnson was not over-fond of music, and the lady was not very skilful. Sensing Johnson's displeasure the lady sought to mollify him:

'Do you know Doctor, that selection was very difficult?'

'Difficult, madam,' retorted Johnson, 'I would to heaven it had been impossible.'

Mozart was visited by a young musician who begged him to explain how to write a symphony.

'You are very young,' said Mozart kindly. 'Why not begin by setting some songs to music?'

'But you composed symphonies when you were only ten years old,' replied the excitable young man.

'True,' admitted Mozart, 'but I never had to ask "how?"'

A young composer was thrilled and flattered when Beethoven came to a performance of his new opera. He was even more delighted when Beethoven approached him after the performance. Anxiously he awaited the verdict:

'I like your opera very much,' said Beethoven, 'in fact I think I shall set it to music one day.'

Beethoven's musical tribute to the Duke of Wellington, *Battle of Victoria*, did not evoke quite the response Beethoven might have hoped for. When asked if the piece had captured the essence of the battle Wellington replied:

'By God, no. If it had been like that I'd have run away myself.'

A violinist had the temerity to complain to Beethoven that the violin part in one of his symphonies was virtually unplayable.

'When I composed that,' Beethoven replied, 'I was conscious of being inspired by God Almighty. Do you think I can consider your puny little fiddle when He speaks to me?'

As Chopin's fame grew the society hostesses of Paris vied with one another to invite him to dinner. It was their irritating habit to expect him to 'sing for his supper' by playing the piano to entertain the other guests after dinner. On one such occasion Chopin declined, explaining:

'But, madame, I have eaten so little.'

Rossini found himself committed to hearing two pieces of music by an aspiring composer and to telling him which he preferred. Patiently Rossini sat through the first piece; but as the eager musician reached for the second score Rossini hastily interrupted him.

'Do not trouble to play further, I find I much prefer the second.'

At a first night party W.S. Gilbert was being plagued by an over-enthusiastic admirer who had clearly heard the maxim that flattery is best laid on with a trowel. Having praised Gilbert to the skies she prepared to laud his collaborator, Sir Arthur Sullivan, in similarly over-familiar terms.

'How wonderful,' she began, 'to think of dear Sir Arthur composing and composing just like Bach.'

'Madam,' interrupted Gilbert, 'Sullivan may be composing but Bach is decomposing.'

Gilbert was adept not just at deflecting compliments but at offering them. After attending a concert by the pianist Liebling he was taken backstage to be introduced. The performance had been rapturously received and Liebling was naturally confident of his visitor's good opinion.

'Sir,' began Gilbert, 'I have heard Liszt,' the pianist nodded expectantly, 'and I have heard Paderewski,' Liebling waited confidently for what was to follow. 'But neither of them,' continued Gilbert, 'perspired as profusely as you do.'

Mark Twain was invited to make up a party at the opera in New York to hear a performance of *La Traviata*. The singing was sublime and everything about the production was perfect but Twain's evening was ruined by his hostess. Delighted to have 'captured' the literary lion she kept up a running whispered commentary to him throughout the evening which he was unable to stem however hard he ignored her. As the curtain came down to tumultuous applause his hostess turned to Twain saying enthusiastically:

'I do hope you will be able to join our party next week, Mr Twain. The opera will be *Tosca*.'

'That would be delightful,' replied Twain gravely, 'I have never heard you in *Tosca* before.'

Jenny Lind, the Swedish nightingale, was world-famous, especially after she was promoted by the American showman P.T. Barnum. Music lovers flocked to see her and often, to her annoyance, came to her home. To one group of devoted admirers who came to her house 'just to see her face' she gave short shrift.

'This is my face,' she said. Then turning her back on them she announced, 'and this is my back,' and left her servant to see them off the premises.

Lilli Lehmann, one of the greatest interpreters of Wagner, was approached during the opening reception of the 1894 Bayreuth festival by another Wagnerian soprano, Lillian Nordica. Miss Nordica asked formally if she might pay Miss Lehmann a call. Putting her rival firmly in her place Miss Lehmann replied:

'I shall not be taking pupils during this season.'

Before his career as a playwright Bernard Shaw was, among other things, a music critic, rejoicing in the *nom de plume* Corno di Bassetto. During a recital by a well-known Italian string quartet a fellow critic spoke highly of the performance, adding, by way of explanation:

'These men have been playing together for twelve years.'

'Surely,' responded Shaw, 'we have been here longer than that.'

Bernard Shaw detested music with his meals – and rightly so. Once he called to the leader of a Tzigane band, which was making the usual deafening and distracting noises in a restaurant:

'Could you play something if I asked you to?'

'But certainly, Monsieur.'

'Well would you either play poker or dominoes – whichever you like – until I have finished my dinner.'

MRS CLAUDE BEDDINGTON
All That I Have Met, 1929

In 1910 Edward VII was entertaining a party to lunch at Buckingham Palace. Below the dining room, in the courtyard, the Guards band played for their entertainment. For some unknown reason their musical director had chosen a seemingly interminable selection from Richard Strauss's tragic and challenging new opera, *Elektra*.

Although the choice was unusual the musicianship was first rate. So their band leader was delighted when the selection came to an end to be given a hand-written note from King Edward himself. Confidently he opened it to read:

'I do not know the *name* of the piece you have just played, but you are *never* to play it again.'

Violinist Fritz Kreisler was asked to perform at a private party and stipulated a sum of $5,000. The client, a society hostess who took the notion of 'Society' very seriously, agreed somewhat reluctantly to the fee and added:

'Of course you will not be expected to fraternize with my guests.'

'In that case,' said Kreisler urbanely, 'the fee is reduced to $2,000.'

Monday 27 March 1939

After Moiseiwitsch had performed at the Savage Club dinner on Saturday night the Vice-Commodore of a famous yacht club said:

'Is that fellah a professional?'
    JAMES AGATE
    A Shorter Ego, 1946

53

Conductor Sir Thomas Beecham, was rehearsing the last act of *La Bohème* and being highly critical of the singer playing Mimi, who could not be heard clearly as she lay dying.

'But Sir Thomas,' protested the harassed artiste, 'one cannot give of one's best in the prone position.'

'I seem to recollect,' replied Beecham, 'that I have given some of my greatest performances while in that position.'

Beecham was conducting a new English opera. The composer attended rehearsals and constantly suggested changes and embellishments. Each time he was interrupted Beecham would listen courteously then turn to the orchestra, lift his baton and say:

'The same again, gentlemen, please.'

I once ventured to compliment Sir Thomas Beecham at a dinner party on his interpretation of Mozart. Sir Thomas thereupon turned to a woman guest and remarked:

'I discuss music only with musicians.'
    JACQUES-EMILE BLANCHE
    More Portraits of a Lifetime, 1939

On Sir Malcolm Sargent's seventieth birthday an ingratiating interviewer from the musical press asked to which particular factor he attributed his long life. The question evoked the well-deserved reply:

'Well, I suppose I must attribute it to the fact that I haven't died yet.'

American baritone Robert Merrill was giving a recital at a university and had been allocated one of the biology laboratories as a private dressing-room. Much to his annoyance a student presented herself during the interval. Assuming her to be an over-enthusiastic admirer Merrill said:

'I never sign autographs during the intermission.'

'Oh I don't want your autograph,' said the young woman, 'I just want to feed my snake.'

Falstaff:	You that are old consider not the capacities of us that are young; you measure the heat of our livers with the bitterness of your galls: and we that are in the vaward of our youth, I must confess, are wags too.
Chief Justice:	Do you set your name down in the scroll of youth, that are written down old with all the characters of age? Have you not a moist eye? a dry hand? a yellow cheek? a white beard? a decreasing leg? and increasing belly? Is not your voice broken? your wind short? your chin double? your wit single? and every part about you blasted with antiquity? and will you yet call yourself young? Fie, fie, fie, Sir John!

WILLIAM SHAKESPEARE
Henry IV, Part 2 (I.2)

The eighteenth-century poet, Alexander Pope, had been stunted by spinal tuberculosis as a child. His intellectual brilliance was matched only by his malicious tendency to ridicule others. On one occasion he sneered at a young man's literary pretensions, asking if he knew what an interrogation was.

'Oh, yes sir,' came the reply, ' 'tis a little crooked thing that asks questions.'

A group of politicians was exchanging banter in the corridors of Westminster. Lord Lauderdale made a joke which greatly amused him, so much so that he was poised to repeat it immediately when Richard Sheridan cut him short saying:

'For God's sake, don't, my dear Lauderdale. A joke in your mouth is no laughing matter.'

The radical politician John Wilkes found himself irritated by a self-important young man who boasted of his talents and achievements during dinner. Even his date of birth appeared to be noteworthy as he declared:

'I was born at mid-day on the first of January. Is that not strange?'

'Not at all', retorted Wilkes. 'You could only have been conceived on the first of April.'

John Wilkes quarrelled with a former friend, the notoriously corrupt 4th Earl of Sandwich. Their quarrel endured for years but gave rise to one of the most celebrated and well-documented snubs. During a chance encounter Sandwich taunted Wilkes, saying:

'Sir, you will either die of the pox or on the gallows.'
Which was neatly countered by Wilkes:

'That depends on whether I embrace your lordship's mistress or your lordship's principles.'

Eighteenth-century French mathemtician d'Alembert had been abandoned at birth and brought up with the family of a glazier named Rousseau. When d'Alembert's fame spread his natural mother returned to reclaim him. D'Alembert rejected her with the words:

'The wife of the glazier is my mother.'

A gentleman expatiating before him on the subject of his mother's beauty, Talleyrand said:

'It must have been your father, then, who was ugly.'

WILLIAM CLARK RUSSELL
The Book of Table-Talk, 1834

The writer Charles Lamb found it necessary to supplement his income for many years by working at the India House. His position was fairly lowly and often irksome. One day an officious superior asked him:

'What are you about, Mr Lamb?'

'About forty,' replied Lamb.

'I like not your answer,' said the man coldly.

'Nor I your question,' replied Lamb, and went back to his work.

When I first knew Charles Lamb, I ventured to say something that should pass for wit.

'Ha! very well, very well, indeed,' said he; 'Ben Jonson has said worse things' (I brightened up, but he went stammering on to the end of the sentence), 'and – and – and *better!*'

A pinch of snuff concluded this compliment, which put an end to my wit for the evening.

JAMES NORTHCOTE
Hazlitt's Conversations with Northcote

Roger Whately, who was Archbishop of Dublin some 175 years ago, was fond of a joke.

'Sir, you are the first man of the age,' said Whately to one whose conceit had offended him.

'Oh, my lord!' replied the other highly delighted; 'you do me too much honour.'

'Not at all,' replied Whately, 'you were born, I believe, in 1801.'

MP and former diplomat Henry Labouchère was enjoying a convivial evening with a crony at his club. The two men were enjoying gossiping and capping each other's racy stories about the great and the good in political and diplomatic circles. Their talk caused much offence to an older club member who eventually rose and went over in high dudgeon.

'Sir,' he accosted Labouchère, 'do you realize that I knew your grandmother?'

'I had no idea,' replied Labouchère gravely, as he rose to his feet. 'Do I perhaps have the honour of addressing my grandfather?'

Society hostess Margot Asquith, wife of Prime Minister Herbert Asquith, was introduced to the film star Jean Harlow. The two famous women eyed one another competitively.

'Margot,' said Jean Harlow, stressing the final 't' of the name heavily, and insolently ignoring the convention of using surnames on introduction, 'how lovely to meet you.'

'My dear,' replied the other crushingly, 'the 't' is silent, as in Harlow.'

Robert Benchley, American writer, and one of the circle of New York wits known as the Algonquin Round Table, emerged from a restaurant, spotted a uniformed man whom he assumed to be the doorman and asked him to call him a cab.

'Sir,' said the offended man, 'I am an Admiral of the United States Navy.'

'In that case,' said Benchley, unperturbed, 'get me a battleship.'

Benchley lived in a hotel for many years. When he finally moved out he left generous gratuities with all the staff, but pointedly ignored the doorman, whom he had found unhelpful.

Hailing Benchley a taxi for the last time the man said:

'Aren't you going to remember me, sir?'

'Of course,' said Benchley, 'I shall write you every day.'

When an arrogant young man told her he couldn't bear fools Dorothy Parker replied:

'How odd. Your mother could apparently.'

'If, sir, I possessed the power of conveying unlimited sexual attraction through the potency of my voice, I would not be reduced to accepting a miserable pittance from the BBC for interviewing a faded female in a damp basement.'

> GILBERT HARDING
> When asked by Mae West's manager 'Can't you sound a bit more sexy when you interview her?'

When introduced to Groucho Marx, an obese matron, comfortably encased in rolls of fat and generously endowed with chins, remarked sociably:

'Oh, how I just adore nature!'

'That's loyalty,' Groucho replied, 'after what nature has done to you.'

A public place near Westminster Abbey
Enter the King and his Train, the Chief-Justice among them

Falstaff: God save thy grace, King Hal; my royal Hal!

Pistol:	The heavens thee guard and keep, most royal imp of fame!
Falstaff:	God save thee, my sweet boy!
King:	My lord chief-justice, speak to that vain man.
Chief-Justice:	Have you your wits? know you what 'tis you speak?
Falstaff:	My king! my Jove! I speak to thee, my heart!
King:	I know thee not, old man: fall to thy prayers;

    How ill white hairs become a fool and jester!

    I have long dream'd of such a kind of man,

    So surfeit swell'd, so old, and so profane;

    But, being awake, I do despise my dream.

    Make less thy body hence, and more thy grace;

    Leave gourmandizing; know thy grave doth gape

    For thee thrice wider than for other men.

    Reply not to me with a fool-born jest:

    Presume not that I am the thing I was;

    For God doth know, so shall the world perceive,

    That I have turn'd away my former self;

    So will I those that keep me company.

WILLIAM SHAKESPEARE
Henry IV, Part 2 (V.5)

Charles James Fox was on the stump during an election and asked a tradesman for his vote. This worthy citizen refused with the neat snub:

'I admire your abilities, but damn ⁝

'And I applaud your sincerity, bu⸝ manners,' riposted Fox.

Henry Clay, a US senator and unsuccessful presidential candidate in 1832 and 1844, was a skilled and inspiring orator. Unfortunately this made him somewhat intolerant of less able speakers. During a boring speech by a fellow senator Clay could be heard complaining about its content and presentation. Stung by the criticism the man turned to him and said:

'You sir, speak for the present generation; but I speak for posterity.'

'Yes,' said Clay, 'and you seem determined to speak until the arrival of your audience.'

One of the Speakers of the House of Representatives towards the end of the nineteenth century was Thomas Brackett Reed. His success in that prestigious office was in large part due to the effective use of his caustic and ready wit. On one occasion a member from the state of Illinois was getting carried away by the justice of his own argument:

'I'm right. I know I am right. So I say, with Henry Clay, sir, "I would rather be right than be President." '

'The gentleman from Illinois will never be either,' said Reed authoritatively.

Making speeches is an integral part of political life. Joseph Chamberlain, while he was Mayor of Birmingham, had to speak at innumerable civic functions. On the whole he found these occasions perfectly agreeable and was flattered to feel that people enjoyed hearing him speak. He was thus rather disconcerted when his host at one event turned to him and said:

'Shall we let them enjoy themselves a little longer, or had we better have your speech now?'

Agnes Macphail, the Canadian suffragette, was being taunted by a male heckler:

'Don't you wish you were a man?'

'Yes,' she shouted back, 'don't you?'

Before becoming President of the United States Woodrow Wilson was Governor of New Jersey. One of the New Jersey senators, a close personal friend, died suddenly. Wilson was deeply upset. Not long after the call with the sad news the telephone rang again. To Wilson's great annoyance the caller, without any preamble, announced:

'Governor, I should like to be first in line to take the senator's place.'

'That's fine by me,' replied Wilson, 'if the undertaker has no objections.'

When F.E. Smith was appointed Lord Chancellor in 1919 one of the first to congratulate him was MP Horatio Bottomley, a brilliant journalist and notorious fraudster who in one short period, between 1901 and 1905, had no fewer than sixty-seven bankruptcy petitions served against him and who had only recently been able to return to the House of Commons.

Commenting on F.E. Smith's meteoric rise to power Bottomley said:

'Upon my soul, F.E., I shouldn't have been surprised to hear that you had been made Archbishop of Canterbury.'

'If I had I should certainly have asked you to my installation,' replied the newly created Lord Chancellor.

'That's uncommonly nice of you,' said Bottomley, aware that his reputation might have debarred him from such an invitation.

'Not at all,' continued Smith. 'I should have needed a crook.'

In 1919, following the First World War, Arthur Balfour was at the Paris Peace Conference presided over by French Prime Minister Clemenceau. The signing of the resulting Treaty of Versailles was naturally surrounded by much ceremony and socializing. At a garden party Clemenceau and Balfour arrived at the same time. Balfour was wearing a top hat but Clemenceau had come in a bowler hat.

'I was told top hats were to be worn,' said Balfour.

'So was I,' returned Clemenceau.

'A man of the utmost insignificance.'
    LORD CURZON
    When asked for his opinion of Baldwin, who had
    become Prime Minister in 1923. Curzon had
    hoped to be Premier

Winston Churchill gave a delicious snub to the ambitious Oswald Mosley, who was thought to get on his feet in the House unduly often.

'I can well understand the hon. member speaking for practice, which he badly needs.'
    EDWARD MARCH
    A Number of People, 1939

Lady Astor was about to go into the House of Commons when she saw a young American sailor lingering outside, apparently uncertain how to gain access. Anxious to assist a compatriot she went over and said:

'If you'd like to go inside I'd be pleased to help.'

Unimpressed by this generous offer he replied:

'You're the sort of broad my mother told me to avoid.'

In 1943 the then Chancellor of the Exchequer, John Simon, anxious to show hospitality to Britain's American allies, showed a party of GIs around the Palace of Westminster. He threw himself into the job with gusto, showing them the Lords and Commons, taking them to areas normally inaccessible to the general public, and even invited them into his private office. His efforts were met in gum-chewing silence and when Simon finally left the group to return to his work one of the GIs turned to Harold Nicolson and asked:

'Say, sir, who *was* that guy?'

Certain politicians cannot resist the opportunity of making an ideological point. Mr Attlee and some colleagues in the post-war Labour government were invited to dine at Buckingham Palace. When the table had been cleared the port was circulated and George VI offered his guests cigars. These were accepted with alacrity except by one man who declined with the pointed remark:

'No thank you, your Majesty. I only smoke cigars on special occasions.'

A fellow MP said to Winston Churchill that Attlee had the virtue of modesty.

'True,' agreed Churchill. 'But then, he does have a lot to be modest about.'

Harold Macmillan's son, the MP Maurice Macmillan, had written a letter to *The Times* criticizing the Conservative government and his father in particular. Dismissing this in the House of Commons Harold Macmillan declared:

'I have never found, in my long experience of politics, that criticism is ever inhibited by ignorance.'

An eager young back-bench MP, fired with enthusiasm for his new calling, and basking in the success of his maiden speech, rose to his feet during Prime Minister's Question Time and asked a brilliant, knock-out question of his leader.

In the corridor afterwards he felt confident of praise as one of the government whips approached him. 'Very good, very good,' he was told, 'but remember what W.G. Grace said to the keen young bowler who got him out with the first ball of the over – "I think you'll find, young man, that they've come to watch *me* bat rather than to see *you* bowl".'

Pinkish toffs like Ian [Gilmour] and Charlie [Morrison], having suffered, for ten years, submission to their social inferior see in Michael [Heseltine] an arriviste, certainly, who can't shoot straight and in Jopling's damning phrase 'bought all his own furniture ...'

    ALAN CLARK
    Diaries 1993 (Saturday 17 November 1990)

I'd rather have a President who screwed women than one who screwed the country.

    SHIRLEY MACLAINE
    When asked whether, as a keen Democrat
    supporter, she was upset by the revelations of John
    F. Kennedy's many extra-marital adventures

Near the door sat Miss Sophy, still fluttered and confused by the attention of Mr Cheggs, and by her side Richard Swiveller lingered for a moment to exchange a few parting words.

'My boat is on the shore and my bark is on the sea, but before I pass this door I will say farewell to thee,' murmured Dick, looking gloomily upon her.

'Are you going?' said Miss Sophy, whose heart sank within her at the result of her stratagem, but who affected a light indifference notwithstanding.

'Am I going!' echoed Dick bitterly. 'Yes, I am. What then?'

'Nothing, except that it's very early,' said Miss Sophy; 'but you are your own master of course.'

'I would that I were my own mistress too,' said Dick, 'before I had ever entertained a thought of you. Miss Wackles, I believed you true, and I was blest in so believing, but now I mourn that e'er I knew, a girl so fair yet so deceiving.'

Miss Sophy bit her lip, and affected to look with great interest after Mr Cheggs, who was quaffing lemonade in the distance.

'I came here,' said Dick, rather oblivious of the purpose with which he had really come, 'with my bosom expanded, my heart dilated, and my sentiments of a corresponding description. I go away with feelings that may be conceived but cannot be described, feeling within myself the desolating truth that my best affections have experienced this night a stifler!'

'I am sure I don't know what you mean, Mr Swiveller,' said Miss Sophy with downcast eyes. 'I'm very sorry if –'

'Sorry, Ma'am!' said Dick, 'sorry in the possession of a Cheggs! But I wish you a very good night, concluding with this slight remark, that there is a young lady growing up at this present moment for me, who has not only great personal attractions but great wealth, and who has requested her next of kin to propose for my hand, which, having regard for some members of her family, I have consented to promise. It's a gratifying circumstance which you'll be glad to hear, that a young and lovely girl is growing into a woman expressly on my account, and is now saving up for me. I thought I'd mention it. I have now merely to apologize for trespassing so long on your attention. Good-night.'

CHARLES DICKENS
The Old Curiosity Shop, 1840–1

Carlton Villa, Teddington,
(Date in full)

My Dear Percy,

Your letter announcing your engagement to Miss —— certainly surprised me. I had no idea that you were contemplating any such step, but I am sure I hope that you have well considered the matter, and that you will not find out, too late, that your ardour has carried you too far.

As for my consent and approval, they do not count. If you had considered me at all you should have asked my opinion before you committed yourself, and then I would have told you that I considered you rash and impulsive. I cannot prevent you being engaged, but I cannot congratulate you upon the step. The young lady is doubtless all you picture her, and I have nothing to urge against her personally. But consent and approval I cannot give. You are too young and inexperienced, too

impecunious, to indulge in such a luxury as a wife for years to come, and a long engagement is a mistake.
I remain,
My dear Percy,
Your affectionate Uncle,
Frank Richards.

> *Beeton's Complete Letter Writer for Ladies and*
> *Gentlemen*

When I am dead, you'll find it hard,
  Said he,
To ever find another man
  Like me.

What makes you think, as I suppose
  You do,
I'd ever want another man
  Like You?
  EUGENE FITCH WARE
  from *The Last Laugh*

During the course of an American tour, Mrs Pat once lost her usual control of the situation. A rather shy, unobtrusive little man was taking her into dinner. She turned her magnetic eyes on him and, in her most effective histrionic tones, said:

'*Tell* me which would *you* sooner do – love passionately or be loved passionately?' The little man took a deep breath, considered, then ventured:

'I'd rather be a canary.'
  MARGARET PETERS
  Mrs Pat: The Life of Mrs Patrick Campbell, 1984

Catherine Howard, fifth wife of Henry VIII, married him at the instigation of relatives anxious to gain political influence. In 1542 the king had her beheaded when he learned of her adultery with Thomas Culpepper. As she stood on the scaffold she took the opportunity of putting the King firmly in his place by declaring:

'I die a Queen, but I would rather die the wife of Culpepper.'

Queen Elizabeth I had a jester, Master Pace, of whom she was very fond and who was allowed to say quite outrageous things as long as they made her laugh. However, on one occasion he over-stepped the mark and was sent away from court for making very personal remarks about the Queen in front of an assembly of foreign dignitaries. Eventually the jester was restored to favour and the Queen welcomed him back with the chiding remark:

'Come now, Pace, let us hear no more of our faults.'

'No indeed Madam,' he replied, 'for I myself never talk of what is discussed by all the world.'

Edward de Vere, Earl of Oxford
This Earle of Oxford, making of his low obeisance to Queen Elizabeth, happened to let a Fart, at which he was so abashed and ashamed that he went to Travell, 7 yeares. On his return the Queen welcomed him home, and say'd, My Lord, I had forgott the Fart.

JOHN AUBREY
Brief Lives

As Elizabeth I was dying she insisted on remaining upright, seated in a chair. Her devoted secretary of state, Robert Cecil, desperately anxious and concerned, insisted she must go to bed.

'Must!' came the scathing response. 'Is "must" a word to be addressed to princes? Little man, little man! Thy father, if he had been alive, durst not have used that word.'

In conversation with Fontenelle, Louis XIV expressed his regret that there seemed so few truly honourable men to be found.

'There are still many honourable men, sire,' replied the philosopher, 'but they do not seek out the society of kings.'

Caroline of Anspach, the admired wife of George II, on her deathbed urged the King to remarry as soon as possible. The distraught King, anxious to comfort her and demonstrate that she was indispensable to him, cried out:

'Never, I shall always take mistresses.'

'That shouldn't hamper your marrying,' she replied, unimpressed.

> Most gracious Queen, we thee implore
> To go away and sin no more.
> But if the effort be too great
> To go away at any rate.
> ANONYMOUS JINGLE
> Current as Caroline of Brunswick was fighting to
> protect her royal status and reputation while
> George IV made an unsuccessful attempt to
> divorce her in 1820

When Alexander II was in Paris following the defeat of Napoleon, he attended anniversary celebrations at one of the hospitals. The ladies who had organized the affair passed plates around for contributions. An extremely pretty girl was delighted to take a plate to the Czar. Alexander dropped in a handful of gold and whispered:

'That's for your beautiful bright eyes.' The young lady curtsied and immediately presented the plate again.

'What? More?' said the Czar.

'Yes, sire,' she replied, 'now I want something for the poor.'

C. SHRINER
Wit, Wisdom, and Foibles of the Great, 1918

Once the Queen heard some gentlemen laughing so loudly at the other end of the room over something one of the party had just related, that she walked across to where they stood, and said, 'I should like to hear that joke Captain——. It must be very amusing.' Captain —— flushed, looked much confused and asked to be exempted from repeating it. The Queen insisted, and the most unfortunate captain, losing his presence of mind, gave it verbatim. It was not a *lady's* joke, and the Queen with much dignity and *hauteur* remarked, 'We are not at all pleased.'

On another occasion, when a number of the Queen's grandchildren, who were visiting her, had got together in their room one of them made a joke which raised such roars of laughter, that Her Majesty entered their apartment to know the cause of such merriment. The joke was somewhat 'advanced', and the young people had to be asked more than once before they could be persuaded to repeat it. But a Queen's command must be obeyed; so the boldest spirit – a masculine one – related it; whereupon Her Majesty drew herself up in dignified rebuke, and with the words 'we are not amused!' left the room.

ARTHUR BEAVAN
Popular Royalty, 1897

A fellow ghillie was talking to Queen Victoria's servant and confidant, John Brown, shortly after the royal party arrived at Balmoral:

'Ye must see a lot o' grand folks in London, John.'

'Me and the Queen pays no attention to them,' was the robust response.

At the time of Edward VII's coronation in 1902 the American painter James McNeill Whistler was in Paris, where he attended a coronation party with a number of other ex-patriots. One of the ladies present said to him:

'I believe you know King Edward, Mr Whistler?'

'No, madam,' he replied.

'How very strange,' she remarked, 'for I met the King last year and I'm sure he told me he knew you.'

'Oh, that was just his brag,' said Whistler.

'They are not royal. They just happen to have me as their aunt.'

ELIZABETH II
On Princess Margaret's children

'I think you will find, Captain, that it is *me* they have come to see.'

ELIZABETH II
To a mounted escort whose horse kept advancing alongside the Queen's coach and obscuring the public's view of her

Prince Philip, Elizabeth II's husband, has earned a reputation for plain speaking which is borne out by the following incident. He arrived by plane at one of the many engagements he fulfills each year. A civic party was waiting to greet him. As so often happens in the presence of a member of the royal family the Mayor was surprised to find himself overcome with nerves and unable to think of a thing to say. Struggling to regain his poise he said the first thing that came into his head:

'How was your flight, your Royal Highness?'

'Have you ever flown?'

'Oh, yes, many times, Sir.'

'Well, it was just like that.'

At a charity gala Fred Astaire was in the line-up to meet the Queen. During their brief encounter he reminded the Queen that he had once danced with her mother, the Queen Mother. This drew the response:

'You mean *she* danced with *you*.'

At a film première Princess Margaret's eye was drawn to the enormous diamond on Elizabeth Taylor's finger.

'That's rather vulgar,' said Her Royal Highness dismissively.

Good-naturedly Miss Taylor persuaded the Princess to try the ring for herself and once it was comfortably fitted on the royal digit remarked:

'There, it's not so vulgar now, is it?'

The 4th Earl of Chesterfield, eighteenth-century politician and wit, was rarely lost for an appropriate response. At one time there was a widely circulated rumour that the courtesan Elizabeth Chudleigh, Countess of Bristol and bigamous Duchess of Kingston, had given birth to illegitimate twins.

'My Lord,' she said to Chesterfield, 'I hope that *you* do not believe the abominable rumours which are circulating about me.'

'Do not distress yourself, madam,' was his reply, 'I rarely believe more than half of what I hear talked of.'

The courtesan Harriet Wilson wrote her memoirs when she found herself short of money. Before publication she approached various former lovers and offered to omit their names for a generous financial consideration. The Duke of Wellington gave her short shrift with the now legendary response:

'Publish and be damned!'

Well past middle age the Austrian Princess Metternich was asked at what age a woman ceases being capable of love.

'You must ask someone else,' replied the princess acidly, 'I am only sixty.'

In the 1890s Lady Veronica McLeod, a general's daughter and noted society beauty, sailed to India to meet her father who was serving with the Indian Army. On the crossing she became attracted to a handsome young steward, second class, and he, not surprisingly, became infatuated with her. In the rarefied atmosphere of a long sea voyage matters became rather heated and they spent a night of illicit passion in her cabin. The young man rose early next day to go about his steward's duties. Some hours later he managed to steal some free time and rushed eagerly to speak to Lady Veronica. Appalled by this social gaucherie she put him firmly back in his place with the words:

'In the circles in which I move, sleeping with a woman does not constitute an introduction.'

Once when Beerbohm Tree came home from a holiday in Paris she [Lady Tree] asked him if he had enjoyed himself.

'Oh, yes, I did, but Paris was thronged with hundreds of appalling Cook's tourists.'

'Ah,' she said, 'I suppose too many Cooks spoiled the brothels.'

> LADY MAUD WARRENDER
> *My First 60 Years*

During a dinner party Bernard Shaw tried the unusual conversational gambit of asking the highly respectable lady on his right if she would consider going to bed with a man for £100,000. Entering into the spirit of the conversation she replied coquettishly that it would rather depend on who the man was and whether or not he were good-looking.

'Would you sleep with a man for five shillings?' Shaw then asked.

'What do you take me for?' she expostulated.

'We have already established that,' said Shaw, 'we are now simply haggling over the price.'

On the second night of his visit, our distingushed guest [Sir Charles Dilke] met Laura in the passage on her way to bed; he said to her:

'If you will kiss me, I will give you a signed photograph of myself.' To which she answered:

'It's awfully good of you Sir Charles, but I would rather not, for what on earth should I do with the photograph?'

> MARGOT ASQUITH
> *Autobiography*, 1922

Dined with Lady Willingdon. Emerald was forty-five minutes late, as she so often and irritatingly is. At one point Emerald, with mischief in her old, over-made up eyes, declared that no man was faithful to his wife for more than three years.

'That,' she added, 'is a biological fact.'

'You can never have known my Freeman,' Lady Willingdon retorted.

'Perhaps better than you think,' was Emerald's reply.
  CHIPS CHANNON
  Diaries (7 December 1942)

During an audition it became clear to comedienne Judy Holliday that the movie mogul interviewing her intended to lure her on to the casting couch. The feeling being far from mutual she stopped him in mid pursuit, reached inside her dress, pulled out her falsies and said:

'Here, I think these are what you're after.'

'I'll send you my bill of fare,' said Lord B. when trying to persuade Dr Swift to dine with him.

'Send me your bill of company,' was Swift's answer to him.
  DR EDWARD YOUNG

To a woman who coquettishly upbraided him with preferring the company of men to that of the fairer sex Dr Johnson responded:

'Madam, I am very fond of the company of ladies. I like their beauty, I like their delicacy, I like their vivacity, and I like their silence.'

Dr Johnson was being drive to distraction at a convivial meal by one particular guest who, anxious to show his acute perception and appreciation of the good Doctor's wit, burst into ostentatious laughter at his every remark. At length Johnson could restrain himself no longer and asked:

'Pray, Sir, what is the matter? I hope I have not said anything that you can comprehend.'

At another dinner Dr Johnson was seated next to an Oxford don who asked him:

'Sir, do you not think that life is often boring?'

'Yes,' replied the Doctor, 'especially if one is sitting next to you.'

Eccentric politician George Augustus Selwyn was so short of entertainment during a spell taking the waters at Bath that he found himself glad of the company of an elderly bore. Unfortunately he then met him by chance when they had both returned to London and Selwyn had more interesting society to cultivate. The old man eagerly approached his friend, saying:

'Sir, do you not remember me?'

'Perfectly, and, when I am next in Bath I shall be happy to renew our acquaintance,' replied Selwyn ruthlessly.

The poet Samuel Rogers was as well known for his wide social acquaintance, ranging from Dr Johnson to William IV, as he was for his poetry. One day at dinner Lady Donegal called across the table to him:

'Now, Mr Rogers, I am sure you are talking about me.'

'Lady Donegal,' he answered, 'I pass my life in defending you.'

SAMUEL ROGERS
Rogers's Table-Talk and Porsoniana, 1856

Regency buck Beau Brummell had an understandable abhorrence of bores. He was put into low spirits one day by the prolonged visit of a man who insisted on telling Brummell, in tedious detail, about his recent tour of the north of England. Eventually the bore, realizing that his listener's attention was wandering, dragged himself from the pleasure of his own monologue and asked Beau Brummell which of the northern lakes he had a preference for. Turning to his valet, Brummel inquired languorously:

'Robinson, which of the lakes do I prefer?'

'Windermere, sir.'

'Windermere,' Brummell informed his visitor. 'So it is, Windermere.'

The naturalist Sir Joseph Banks had a sister, Sarah Sophia, who shared his interest in natural history and who cultivated a certain eccentricity. An unwary visitor remarked:

'It is a fine day, ma'am,' and was put firmly in his place.

'I know nothing at all about it. You must speak to my brother upon that subject when you are at dinner.'

Sydney Smith:	May I ask you what procures me the honour of this visit?
Visitor:	Oh, I am compounding a history of the distinguished families in Somersetshire, and have called to obtain the Smith arms.
Sydney Smith:	I regret, sir, not to be able to contribute to so valuable a work; but the Smiths never had any arms, and have invariably sealed their letters with their thumbs.

'Shall I go away, aunt?' I asked, trembling.

'No, sir,' said my aunt. 'Certainly not!' With which she pushed me into a corner near her, and fenced me in with a chair, as if it were a prison or a bar of justice. This position I continued to occupy during the whole interview, and from it I saw Mr and Miss Murdstone enter the room.

'Oh!' said my aunt, 'I was not aware at first to whom I had the pleasure of objecting. But I don't allow anybody to ride over that turf. I make no exceptions. I don't allow anybody to do it.'

'Your regulation is rather awkward to strangers,' said Miss Murdstone.

'Is it!' said my aunt.

Mr Murdstone seemed afraid of a renewal of hostilities, and interposing began: 'Miss Trotwood!'

'I beg your pardon,' observed my aunt with a keen look. 'You are the Mr Murdstone who married the widow of my late nephew, David Copperfield, of Blunderstone Rookery! – Though why Rookery, *I* don't know!'

'I am,' said Mr Murdstone.

'You'll excuse my saying, sir,' returned my aunt, 'that I think it would have been a much better and happier thing if you had left that poor child alone.'

'I so far agree with what Miss Trotwood has remarked,' observed Miss Murdstone, bridling, 'that I consider our lamented Clara to have been, in all essential respects, a mere child.'

'It is a comfort to you and me, ma'am,' said my aunt, 'who are getting on in life, and are not likely to be made unhappy by our personal attractions, that nobody can say the same of us.'

CHARLES DICKENS
David Copperfield, 1849–50

A fellow guest observed Anthony Trollope at dinner taking large helpings of everything on offer and remarked rather pointedly:

'You seem to have an excellent appetite, Mr Trollope.'

'Not at all, madam, but, thank God, I am very greedy,' he replied, neatly drawing attention to the offensive nature of her observation.

American writer Mark Twain and fellow-novelist William Dean Howells were leaving church one Sunday morning when the heavens opened and there was a sudden downpour of rain.

'Do you think it will stop?' asked Howells.

'It always has,' said Twain.

An American lady visiting London struck up a conversation with her compatriot, the eminent artist James Whistler, at a reception.

'Where were you born, Mr Whistler,' she inquired, anxious to place his antecedents.

'In Lowell, Massachusetts,' he replied.

'Why, Mr Whistler, whatever possessed you to be born in such a place?' she exclaimed coquettishly.

'The explanation is quite simple,' came the solemn reply. 'I wished to be near my mother.'

Oscar Wilde went into a florist's shop and asked:

'Can you take flowers out of the window?'

'Certainly, sir,' said the eager assistant, 'which ones would you like?'

'Oh, I don't want to buy any. I simply thought some of them looked rather tired.'

I am getting quite accustomed to being snubbed by Lupin, and I do not mind being sat upon by Carrie, because I think she has a certain amount of right to do so; but I do think it hard to be at once snubbed by wife, son, and both my guests.

Gowing and Cummings had dropped in during the evening, and I suddenly remembered an extraordinary dream I had a few nights ago, and I thought I would tell them about it. I dreamt I saw some huge blocks of ice in a shop with a bright glare behind them. I walked into the shop and the heat was overpowering. I found that the blocks of ice were on fire. The whole thing was so real and yet so supernatural I woke up in a cold perspiration. Lupin in a most contemptuous manner, said: 'What utter rot.'

Before I could reply, Gowing said there was nothing so completely uninteresting as other people's dreams.

I appealed to Cummings, but he said he was bound to agree with the others and my dream was especially nonsensical. I said: 'It seemed so real to me.' Gowing replied: 'Yes, to *you* perhaps, but not to *us*.' Whereupon they all roared.

Carrie, who had hitherto been quiet, said: 'He tells me his stupid dreams every morning nearly.' I replied: 'Very well, dear, I promise you I will never tell you or anybody else another dream of mine the longest day I live.' Lupin said: 'Hear! hear!' and helped himself to another glass of beer. The subject was fortunately changed, and Cummings read a most interesting article on the superiority of the bicycle to the horse.

GEORGE AND WEEDON GROSSMITH
The Diary of a Nobody, 1892

Trapped by a club bore Lord Randolph Churchill was desperate to escape. Seeing one of the club servants he called him over and instructed him:

'Listen until his lordship finishes,' then beat a hasty retreat.

At a party for a private view an enthusiastic admirer bore down upon Whistler and tried to start up a conversation:

'Oh, Mr Whistler, you know only the other day I passed your house and …'

'Thank you,' said Whistler and moved swiftly on.

William R. Travers, an American lawyer known for both his stammer and his ready wit, had been seated next to a dreary and opinionated man during dinner. The man eventually felt it was time to draw Travers into the conversation and, referring to the earlier part of the meal, asked:

'Do you think that oysters have brains?'

'Y-y-yes,' replied Travers pointedly, 'J-j-j-just enough b-b-b-brains to k-keep their m-mouths sh-sh-shut.'

When the Women's Institute started at the turn of the century, they were determined to cross class barriers. One president remarked with satisfaction: 'We have done very well; we have elected five ladies, five women and one school-teacher.'

    SIMON GOODENOUGH
    Jam and Jerusalem

Horatio Bottomley went to see Lord Cholmondley. When the butler answered the door Bottomley announced:

'I have come to see Lord Chol-mond-ley.'

'Lord *Chum*ley,' said the butler patronizingly.

'All right then,' said Bottomley, unabashed, 'tell him it's Mr Bumley to see him.'

Grace Vanderbilt was required to give precedence to Nancy Astor at a dinner given by President Theodore Roosevelt. To console her Nancy explained:

'Of course, the Astors skinned skunks a hundred years before the Vanderbilts worked ferries.'

An acquaintance accosted Asquith's daughter, Lady Violet Bonham-Carter, at a reception:
'We went to the Savoy Grill the other day for luncheon but we were very disappointed.'
'Oh, why was that?'
'Well, I don't think they quite knew who we were.'
Lady Violet: 'Really! And who were you?'

Mrs Patrick Campbell had spent most of dinner listening to the man on her left, an eminent biologist, talking about his life's work and obsession – ants. After more than an hour on the topic he confided enthusiastically:
'They even have their own army and their own police force.'
'Indeed,' said Mrs Pat, 'no navy I suppose?'

Mrs Pat's friend, Bernard Shaw, suffered a similarly dreary dinner which was quite ruined by the interminable and opinionated conversation of the man next to him. When he finally drew breath Shaw took the opportunity to remark gently:
'You know, between us we know everything there is to be known.'
'How is that?' asked his neighbour, basking in the welcome compliment.
'Well, you see,' continued Shaw, 'you know everything except the fact that you are a bore, and I know that!'

Bernard Shaw passionately disliked the company of social climbers who 'collected' well-known people. An invitation from one such hostess arrived in the form of an At Home card worded:

'Mrs ——— ———, At Home, Thursdays 4 o'clock until 5 o'clock.'

Shaw wrote underneath:

'Mr Bernard Shaw likewise,' and promptly returned it whence it came.

Isabella Gardner, a New Yorker who married into the élite of Boston society, resented the unwelcoming behaviour she suffered from the most die-hard snobbish elements. Tired of hearing them constantly boasting of their ancestors' arrival from England on the *Mayflower* she one day allowed herself the luxury of observing:

'Indeed! I understand the immigration laws are much stricter nowadays.'

Calvin Coolidge, thirtieth President of the United States and famous for the statement 'The business of America is business', was not known for his social graces. After speaking at a fund-raising dinner, he was approached by an enthusiastic lady supporter.

'Mr President,' she gushed, 'you were too, too wonderful. I arrived late and I couldn't find a seat but do you know, I stood up through your entire speech.'

'So did I, madam,' said Coolidge.

A lady seated next to the taciturn Calvin Coolidge at dinner one evening confided:

'Mr President, I have taken a wager that I can get at least three consecutive words from you tonight.'

To which Coolidge replied:

'You lose.'

Many people were anxious to make the acquaintance of T.E. Lawrence – the enigmatic war hero Lawrence of Arabia. At an embassy party in Egypt he found himself approached by a persistent celebrity head-hunter. Seizing on the perennial topic of the weather and the sweltering heat he endeavoured to strike up a conversation:

'Ninety-two today, Colonel Lawrence! Think of that! ninety-two.'

'Congratulations and many happy returns,' replied Lawrence, and made his escape.

Nancy Astor hosted delightful weekend parties at her stately home, Cliveden. To one of these parties Jimmy Thomas, a Labour MP. was invited. Nancy Astor asked him what subject he would choose if she asked him to address the assembled party.

'I shall tell them what a Socialist government will do with this house when it gets into power,' was the rather ungracious reply.

'*My* suggestion,' replied Lady Astor, unperturbed, 'would be to turn it into a boarding-house and me into a landlady. Of course in that case, Mr Thomas, you would be expected to pay for your board and lodging, which you have never done in the past.'

Mr Astor, having built a new patio for his house with tiles bought from Segovia proudly showed it to Mrs Stuyvesant Fish.

In the centre of the patio was a large fountain. With an air of pride he waited for her to express admiration.

'Beautiful,' said Mrs Fish, her head on one side. 'Beautiful! Just the sort of watering trough one might put up for a favourite horse.'

ELIZABETH, LADY DECIES
Turn of the World, 1938

Later in life I had a beautiful object-lesson in behaviour to the unpunctual. The scene was a luncheon party at the Broughams': the appointed time, 1.30. Till 1.45 we waited for Lady Cunard; and at two o'clock she arrived, full of apologies – she had been buying a chandelier. Old Lord Brougham, a handsome patriarch with magnificent silver hair, looked straight in front of himself and said in a pensive tone:

'I once knew a man who bought a chandelier *after* luncheon.'

EDWARD MARSH
A Number of People, 1939

'I am not really a London person,' said Sir Leicester, reproachfully. 'I work in London, but my home is in Surrey.'

'I count that,' Aunt Sadie said, gently but firmly, 'as the same.'

NANCY MITFORD
The Pursuit of Love, 1945

Ernest Thesiger, a genial actor of the old school, was a guest at a very smart but very dull party. Wandering around the building looking for someone to talk to he came into the library, where a pleasant-looking man, who looked vaguely familiar, was standing alone by the fire. Thesiger approached him and attempted to break the ice by introducing himself:

'Hello. My name's Ernest. I'm an actor.'

Back came the unsettling reply:

'Hello, my name's George. I'm a king.'

Making small talk is fraught with pitfalls as one struggles to fill the social vacuum with desultory chat. Pity then the poor man who, casting around for something to say, asked Groucho Marx if Groucho was his real name.

'No,' replied Groucho, 'it's not my name at all. I'm breaking it in for a friend.'

Groucho Marx also coined the classic snub, to a woman at a party who insisted they had met before:

'I never forget a face, but in your case I'll make an exception.'

Dame Barbara Cartland, staunch upholder of traditional values and romantic novelist supreme, found herself part of a real-life fairy-tale romance when Lady Diana Spencer, her own daughter's step-daughter, married the Prince of Wales in 1981. Naturally Miss Cartland, as she then was, was much in demand for media interviews. On one of these occasions she was asked whether or not she thought class barriers were broken down in modern Britain.

'Of course, otherwise I wouldn't be here talking to someone like you,' was her reply.

The story is told that at one of Miss Cartland's dinner parties, immediately after the first course, a guest had the temerity to ask whether she would mind if he smoked.

'Not at all,' said Miss Cartland, sweetly, 'I shall instruct the butler to cancel the rest of the meal.'

In one of Dryden's plays there was this line, which the actress endeavoured to speak in as moving and affecting a tone as she could:

'My wound is great because it is so small!'
and then she paused, and looked very much distressed. The Duke of Buckingham, who was in one of the boxes, rose from his seat, and added in a loud ridiculing voice:

'Then, 'twould be greater were it none at all!'

which had so strong an effect on the audience (who before were not very well pleased with the play) that they hissed the poor woman off the stage, would never bear her appearance in the rest of her part, and (as this was the second time only of the play's appearance) made Dryden lose his benefit night.

DR FRANCIS LOCKIER

On the first performance of one of Voltaire's tragedies, the success of which was very equivocal, the Abbé Pellegrin complained loudly that Voltaire had stolen some verses from him.

'How can you, who are so rich,' said he, 'thus seize upon the property of another?'

'What!' replied Voltaire, 'have I stolen from you? I no longer wonder that my piece has met with so little approbation.'

DOM CHAUDON
Memoirs of M. Voltaire, 1786

The French tragedienne Rachel was boasting to a less successful colleague of her most recent theatrical triumph:

'When I made my entrance the audience sat there completely open-mouthed.'

'Not possible,' replied the other actress, 'they never all yawn at exactly the same time.'

An aspiring playwright sent a script of his new play to the actor-manager Sir Herbert Beerbohm Tree, asking for his opinion, and not unhopeful of a positive response. Back came Tree's reply:

My Dear Sir,
I have read your play. Oh, my dear Sir!

Yours faithfully etc.,

Beerbohm Tree

Rehearsing a new production at His Majesty's Theatre Beerbohm Tree asked one of the young actors playing a minor part to step back upstage. This he did, the director scribbled on his text and the rehearsal continued. A few minutes later Beerbohm Tree again requested the young man to step back. The actor complied, again the director marked his script and the rehearsal continued once more. A short time later Beerbohm Tree stopped the proceedings a third time and asked the young man to step back even further.

'But if I do that I will be right off the stage,' he protested.

'That's right,' said Beerbohm Tree equably, and returned to studying his script.

We are used to the concept that the actor must try to please the critics and the audience, but actors do not always view the process as one-way traffic. John Barrymore, who had endured several nights in competition with audiences who snuffled, sneezed and had fits of uncontrolled barking coughing, came onstage, threw a fish out into the stalls and called out:

'Busy yourselves with that, you damned walruses, while the rest of us proceed with the play.'

A frequent member of the company in Gilbert and Sullivan's comic operas was the actor George Grossmith, who achieved lasting fame himself as the co-author of *The Diary of a Nobody*. He and Gilbert did not always see eye to eye but even a Grossmith found it difficult to get the better of Gilbert's quick wit. During a rehearsal of *Iolanthe* in 1882 Gilbert caught Grossmith complaining to another member of the cast.

'What did you say, Mr Grossmith?' inquired Gilbert.

'I was simply saying, Mr Gilbert, that we have rehearsed this so many times that by now I feel a perfect fool.'

'Well, perhaps we can now talk on equal terms,' said Gilbert.

'I beg your pardon?' said Grossmith, surprised.

'I accept your apology,' replied Gilbert, and resumed the rehearsal.

Wm. Wheatleigh Esq.,
Manager,
New York City.

Dear Sir,

This will introduce the eminent tragedian Mr McKean Buchanen. He wants to play in New York. I have seen him play Macbeth, Richelieu and poker. He plays the latter best.

Yours etc. C.W. Couldock
    quoted in *Shop Talk* by Milton Nobles

Young actors learning their craft the hard way is a well established theatrical tradition. Sir Henry Irving, Britain's first theatrical knight, ran the Lyceum theatre, overseeing every detail of the productions himself. In 1882 he put on *Romeo and Juliet*. A group of young actors, anxious to make their mark, threw themselves energetically into rehearsals for one of the fight scenes between the Montagus and the Capulets. There was much leaping, spinning, wrestling and clashing of swords as the young people gave their all in pursuit of realism. Irving watched their undisciplined cavortings patiently for some minutes before halting the proceedings with the damning remark:

'Very good, gentlemen, very good. But please – don't fidget.'

Ellen Terry was appearing in a play directed by the young Dion Boucicault, son of the playwright. Directors were something of an innovation at the end of the nineteenth century; in the past actors had always directed themselves. The young Boucicault had prepared very thoroughly and mapped out moves and gestures in painstaking detail. Miss Terry was not inclined to prima donna behaviour but after enduring several hours of rehearsal to which she was unable to contribute any of her great experience and talent she moved towards the footlights and addressed the callow young director:

'And pray tell me, Mr Boucicault, when do you want me to do that little extra something for which you are paying me all this money?'

Mrs Patrick Campbell, leading actress of her day and close friend of Bernard Shaw, was constantly at loggerheads with one of her producers, Charles Froham. Her exit line as she swept from the room after one of their explosive rows was:

'Always remember, Mr Froham, that I am an artist.'

'Your secret is safe with me,' he called after her.

In 1896 Mrs Pat found herself trapped with Henry Arthur Jones who read through the entire text of his new play, *Michael and the Lost Angel* in his native

Buckinghamshire accent. When he finished, after several wearying hours, she rose and left with just one comment:

'But it's so very long, Mr Jones – even *without* the aitches.'

One of the most amusing stage 'knock-outs' I know is the one recounted by Ben Travers which was delivered to him by Charles Hawtrey. The great man had been engaged to direct Travers' first farce, *The Dippers*, and the nervous young playwright had been summoned to attend the first rehearsal. To his horror he arrived to find Hawtrey systematically working his way through the best scene in the play with a red pencil, cutting great chunks out of the dialogue. Travers stood there timidly watching, as his brain-child was gradually whittled away. Finally the pencil point came to his favourite line in the play, halted momentarily, and then struck through it.

'Oh, Mr Hawtrey,' exclaimed Travers, 'that last line. Must that go? I'm sorry, but really I always thought that was rather a good line.'

'A good line?' repeated Hawtrey slowly, 'a good line? It's a very good line indeed, dear boy. You mustn't on any account lose it. Put it in another play.'

KENNETH WILLIAMS
Acid Drops, 1980

Lilian Baylis, the formidable founder of the Old Vic theatre company, ran a very tight ship. Relationships were discouraged between people in her company. Despite this a young actor and actress dared to approach her, albeit timidly, with the news that they were in love and wished to get married.

'Go away,' said Miss Baylis, 'I don't have time to listen to gossip.'

Outrageous American star Tallulah Bankhead was approached by an enthusiastic young actress.

'Miss Bankhead,' she breathed, 'I want to become an actress and devote my life to American theatre.'

'If you really want to help American theatre, darling,' drawled Tallulah, 'be an audience.'

Lynn Fontanne was approached by Tallulah Bankhead:

'How lucky you are to be married to Alfred Lunt, darling. His directing, his acting, his theatre sense. Where would you be without it?'

'Probably playing your parts, darling,' replied Miss Fontanne.

James Agate was talking to Lilian Braithwaite at a party. Hoping to excite her professional jealousy and curiosity he declared:

'I have been wanting to tell you for a long time that I regard you as the second best actress in London.'

Refusing to rise to the bait Miss Braithwaite replied charmingly:

'I am deeply flattered to hear that from the second best theatre critic in London.'

After the making of the film *Bill of Divorcement* Katharine Hepburn turned to her leading man, John Barrymore:

'Thank God I don't have to act with you any more!'

'I wasn't aware you ever had,' was his reply.

The long relationship of Katharine Hepburn and Spencer Tracy has been well documented. Yet at their meeting before making their first film together each was wary of the other's reputation. Miss Hepburn went into the attack first:

'I'm afraid I'm a little tall for you, Mr Tracy.'

'Don't worry about that, Miss Hepburn,' came the reply. 'I'll soon cut you down to size.'

As a young woman society hostess Lady Diana Cooper scored an acting success as a statue in Max Reinhardt's sentimental religious play, *The Miracle*. Some twenty years later, Lady Diana, in an unguarded moment, said somewhat dismissively to Noel Coward, who was at the height of his fame:

'Didn't you write *Private Lives*? Not very funny.'

To which Noel replied:

'Weren't you in *The Miracle*? Very funny indeed.'

A producer, who had rejected one of Bernard Shaw's early plays, changed his mind when Shaw began to achieve success. A telegram was sent with an offer to produce the play. This allowed Shaw the pleasure of sending a crisp reply in return:

'Better never than late.'

Bernard Shaw sent Winston Churchill two tickets for the first night of one of his plays, with the message:

'Bring a friend – *if* you have one.'

Churchill telegraphed an immediate response:

'Can't come to first night STOP Will come to second, if you have one.'

An actress sent a telegram to Bernard Shaw:

'Am crazy to play St Joan'

Bernard Shaw despatched a telegram in reply:

'I quite agree'

But in another exchange of telegrams Shaw found himself outclassed snub for snub. His correspondent was American actress Cornelia Otis Skinner who was enjoying great success in Shaw's *Candida* on Broadway in 1935. Shaw sent her a congratulatory message:

'Excellent! Greatest!'

Back came the reply:

'A million thanks but undeserving such praise'

Shaw sent a further telegram:

'I meant the play'

Which Miss Skinner capped with:

'So did I'

Director Tyrone Guthrie was a stickler for detail and, quite rightly, despised sloppy presentation, even among the lowliest of the walk-on parts. At the dress rehearsal of *The Thrie Estates*, which he directed at the 1948 Edinburgh Festival, he paraded the crowd scene actors in a last minute inspection for careless anachronisms such as wristwatches. One young man, desperately anxious to please, had gone to town with his theatrical make-up, showing too much, rather than too little attention to detail. Confident of passing muster he was appalled to hear Guthrie observe:

'Ah, now here's a young lad who's made himself up as a flag.'

Edith Evans, on the opening night of Christopher Fry's verse drama *The Dark is Light Enough* at the Aldwych theatre in 1954, swept off to her dressing-room as the curtain fell on the first act, calling over her shoulder to her leading man, James Donald:

'Mr Donald, you don't have to win you know. We are both on the same side.'

Noel Coward was accosted in the street by a fan.

'You remember me, surely,' persisted the woman, 'I

met you with Douglas Fairbanks.'

'Madam,' replied Coward, 'I don't even remember Douglas Fairbanks.'

In order to jolly up my rather shabby and bare dressing room, I put up one of those large and rather garish posters of a Spanish bull on the inside of my door. One night Noel [Coward] came round with his friend Graham Payn, the actor, to see me. I always felt rather nervous in the Master's presence, because in his later years he could be quite irascible. We were talking fairly easily when there was suddenly one of those awful pauses when you feel you have to say something. In desperation I pointed to the poster and said:

'I got that in Spain.' To which he immediately replied:

'I didn't think you got it in Aberdeen.'

RICHARD BRIERS

Coward and Company, 1987

Bishop Burnet's absence of mind is well known. Dining with the Duchess of Marlborough, after her husband's disgrace, he compared this great general to Belisarius.

'But,' said the Duchess eagerly, 'how came it that such a man was so miserable and universally detested?'

'Oh, Madam!' (exclaimed the *distrait* prelate) 'he had such a brimstone of a wife!'

HORACE WALPOLE